"Almost every word, phrase, or sentence written by Gerhard Lohfink was worth reading. With his landmark book *Jesus of Nazareth*, he firmly established himself as one of the most influential and inspiring New Testament scholars of our age. In his final book, he shares the moving story of his coming of age and his coming into an adult faith. By turns surprising, challenging, and profound, Lohfink's memoir will renew, restore, or revitalize your own Christian faith."

— James Martin, SJ, author of *Jesus: A Pilgrimage* and *Learning to Pray*

"Part autobiography, part theology, *Why I Believe in God* is theologian Gerhard Lohfink's final gift to the world. Whether he is unpacking the notoriously difficult concept of original sin or describing what it was like to grow up Catholic in Nazi Germany, his writing is marked by the wry wisdom, gentle love, and humble courage of a true disciple—one whose life was in every way a mirror of his deep faith. This book moved me to tears."

— Paula Huston, author of *The Hermits of Big Sur* and *One Ordinary Sunday: A Meditation on the Mystery of the Mass*

"A distinguished professor of New Testament, the late Gerhard Lohfink's *Why I Believe in God* is less autobiography than what he calls an 'appropriate theology.' Against the background of growing up in Nazi Germany and the devastation of the war, he tells of discerning his vocation as priest and career as a scholar as he explores important subjects such as God, Trinity, original sin, canon, community, and Church, so often misunderstood or dismissed in our secular age. This creative apologetics is an insightful and engaging read."

— Thomas P. Rausch, SJ, Emeritus T. Marie Chilton Chair of Catholic Theology, Loyola Marymount University

"Gerhard Lohfink has been a significant voice in my ongoing development as a scholar and person of faith. After reading so many of his academic works, what a joy to finally come to know him as a person in this final work. *Why I Believe in God* is not a systematic argument for the existence of God, but the story of a life lived in relationship with God as found in a community of Christian believers. This book is not a text but a testimony."

— Ann M. Garrido, associate professor of homiletics, Aquinas Institute of Theology

Gerhard Lohfink

Why I Believe in God

Translated by

Linda M. Maloney

LITURGICAL PRESS
Collegeville, Minnesota

litpress.org

Cover illustration by Br. Martin Erspamer, OSB, a monk of Saint Meinrad Archabbey, Indiana. Used with permission.

Library of Congress Cataloging-in-Publication Data

Names: Lohfink, Gerhard, 1934–2024, author. | Maloney, Linda M., translator.
Title: Why I believe in God / Gerhard Lohfink ; translated by Linda M. Maloney.
Other titles: Warum ich an Gott glaube. English
Description: Collegeville, Minnesota : Liturgical Press, [2025] | Includes bibliographical references and index. | Translated from the German. | Summary: "Why do I believe in God? That is the question renowned Scripture scholar, Gerhard Lohfink answers in this, his final "biography of faith." In Why I Believe in God, Lohfink reflects on the light of faith he received through the church, and his desire to bring it together anew with the light of his own reason. Through personal, biblical, and theological reflections, Lohfink offers readers a glimpse into his own story of faith"— Provided by publisher.
Identifiers: LCCN 2024051805 (print) | LCCN 2024051806 (ebook) | ISBN 9780814689974 (hardcover) | ISBN 9780814689981 (epub) | ISBN 9798400802218 (pdf)
Subjects: LCSH: Lohfink, Gerhard, 1934–2024. | Catholic Church—Clergy—Biography. | New Testament scholars—Germany—20th century—Biography. | Faith (Christianity)—Catholic Church.
Classification: LCC BX4705.L687 A3 2025 (print) | LCC BX4705.L687 (ebook) | DDC 282.092 [B]—dc23/eng/20241213
LC record available at https://lccn.loc.gov/2024051805
LC ebook record available at https://lccn.loc.gov/2024051806

Rudolf Schnackenburg
In Memoriam

Contents

Preface

I love autobiographies. There are dozens of them on my bookshelves. At the same time, I hate them. I love them because many authors give a poignant and even thrilling account of the first twenty or thirty years of their lives. But then the autobiography gradually morphs into the second part, in which the author (now famous) mainly tells of all the many other famous people he or she has encountered during his or her lifetime.

This book is not an autobiography. I am not interested in telling about exciting *public* events in my lifetime. There were none. My subject, rather, is how an ordinary person can come to faith. For that purpose I refer to my own life, but only small segments of it, often with rapid transitions in time. This is not a reminiscence about my own life; it is about an appropriate theology. More precisely: I want to consider how Christian faith can exist in a world filled with hatred, war, and destruction. In such a world, is it still possible to believe in God?

The title of this book draws deliberately on the Apostles' Creed, which begins:

I believe in God

The basic form of this creed was already known in the second century CE.[1] But for what purpose was it created? Its *Sitz im Leben* was not originally Sunday worship, but the baptismal liturgy at the Easter Vigil.

[1] One of the oldest forms is found in the twenty-first chapter of the *Traditio Apostolica*, attributed to Hippolytus (44–59). See Paul F. Bradshaw, *Apostolic Tradition: A New Commentary* (Collegeville, MN: Liturgical Press, 2023). For the whole subject see the fundamental work of J. N. D. Kelly, *Early Christian Creeds: History and Theology* (London: Longman, Green & Co., 1950).

The baptizands—at first nearly all were adults—did not simply recite the creed as a continuous text. Instead, their creed was part of a dialogue.[2] More precisely: the three parts of the creed were presented as questions to the individual baptizands:

Do you believe in God [. . .] ?

Do you believe in Jesus Christ [. . .] ?

Do you believe in the Holy Spirit [. . .] ?

My ellipses are used to make it clear that the whole creed was presented to the baptizands in this three-part form, and each individual answered three times: "I do believe." After each "I do believe," the baptizand, who was standing in a river or in a pool in a baptistry, was submerged or at least sprinkled with water.[3]

This dialogical structure of the creed is preserved today in many Christian baptismal rites, and above all in the annual renewal of the baptismal promises during the Easter Vigil. Likewise retained is "*I* believe." In the Roman Catholic celebration of the Easter Vigil, for example, the priest asks the assembled congregation:

Do you believe in God, the Father, the Almighty, maker of heaven and earth?

[. . .]

Of course we expect the response to be "*we* believe," but instead, remarkably, the answer each time is "*I* believe," and so with the

[2] The technical term is "interrogatories"—that is, the creed was presented in question form, and not simply recited in "declaratory" fashion by the baptizands.

[3] Cf. *Didachē* 7.1-3:

(1) As for baptism, baptize in this way:

Having said all this beforehand, baptize in the name of the Father and of the Son and of the Holy Spirit, in running water.

(2) If you (sg. through vv. 2-4) do not have running water, however, baptize in another kind of water; if you cannot [do so] in cold [water], then [do so] in warm [water].

(3) But if you have neither, pour water on the head thrice in the name of Father and Son and Holy Spirit.

Kurt Niederwimmer, *The Didachē*, trans. Linda M. Maloney, Hermeneia (Minneapolis: Fortress Press, 1998), 125.

next two questions! Thus, as in the early Christian celebration of baptism, each participant is addressed *as an individual*, and each, in saying "I believe," makes a personal confession of faith.

But above all—and this is what is most important to me here: inasmuch as the whole event takes place in the church and is carried out as a dialogue between priest and people, it is clear that we cannot produce faith out of ourselves. We receive it from God—mediated through Jesus Christ and the church.[4] Still, each individual must also receive it with her or his whole existence and confess it.

The basic structure of this book follows that model. I want to speak about my personal faith in God—hence the embedded autobiographical bits—but not as something I myself have organized and put together. Instead, I want to write about what I have "received"[5]—and for which I have been held accountable again and again throughout my life.

In other words: I am telling about the light of faith that God has given me, through the church—but which I have repeatedly had to bring together anew with the light of my reason and that of the world.

Why do I believe in God? My answer is given in fourteen steps: fourteen chapters. They are solidly connected with my own life-history. In the lives of other Christians this "biography of faith" will probably look different in many respects. In principle it is different for every Christian. Each of us has her or his own story of faith—or of not being able to believe.

One other aside: This book is based in large part on a talk I gave in 2017 at Wangen in the Allgäu; it was documented in my book *Im Ringen um die Vernunft. Reden über Israel, die Kirche, und die*

[4] This is clear not only from the dialogical structure of questions and answers. The mere fact that infant baptism has come to prevail throughout Christianity (except in certain groups) points to the nature of faith as a gift. [The structure here described is also that of the Easter Vigil rite in the *Book of Common Prayer* (ECUSA), 292–94; the same Baptismal Covenant is recited by the congregation at every celebration of Baptism and on several feasts throughout the church year, in the same interrogatory form.]—Tr.

[5] For this "reception" of faith in the NT see especially 1 Cor 15:3; Gal 1:9; Phil 4:9; Col 2:6; 1 Thess 2:13; 2 Thess 3:6.

Europäische Aufklärung.[6] That previous text has not only been revised and expanded here in many places; it has also been essentially extended, up to our hard-pressed present, an era that makes it more and more difficult for many Christians to believe in a God who is and remains the ruler of history.

I dedicate this book in profound gratitude to my teacher and Doktorvater, Professor Rudolf Schnackenburg (1914–2002).

[6] Freiburg: Herder, 2016, 495–518. This work will be published in English translation by Liturgical Press in 2026 as *The Light of Faith and Reason: Israel, Jesus, and the Enlightenment*. Some chapters have been omitted from that book because they can be found in this one, including "Why I Believe in God," referred to here.

1

My Parents' House

So, why do I believe in God? The first answer is simply: because *my parents* believed in God. That means: without being able to do anything about it, I grew up in a Christian family in which it was simply a matter of course that I was baptized a week after I was born, and then I received a Christian upbringing.

Had I been born in Jordan I would probably have been a Muslim. If I came from Thailand or Cambodia I would almost certainly be a Buddhist now. If born in Japan I would probably visit a Shinto shrine from time to time and forge a spiritual connection with my ancestors and the Japanese homeland.[1] But I had Roman Catholic parents and therefore I became a Catholic Christian. A statistician would call it a demographic accident. I call it grace.

It was likewise pure grace that my mother and father were not only baptized Christians but people who lived their faith. Morning prayer, evening prayer, prayers before and after meals, attendance at Mass on Sundays, occasional household devotions, the observance of feastdays and liturgical seasons, the solemn celebration of First Communion: all that—at least from the children's point of view—was a matter of course in our family.

Unforgettable for me were the annual Christmas Eve observances. In the years before 1944, at a time when we had not yet been bombed out and still had a spacious rented house, the door

[1] Cf. Ama Toshimaro, *Why Are the Japanese Non-Religious? Japanese Spirituality: Being Non-Religious in a Religious Culture*, trans. Ama Michihiro (Lanham, MD: University Press of America, 2005).

to the so-called "best room," where we only ate our meals on feastdays, was closed. Inside that room our mother had made all the preparations for Christmas Eve and was now putting on the final touches. We children sat in the living room with our father and waited. At some point, then, the door opened, and all eyes focused on the decorated Christmas tree. But it was not just our eyes that were entranced: the air was filled with the smell of evergreens and candles.

Of course our gaze was then also drawn to the gifts, but those were covered by a white tablecloth and our furtive glances could only discern mysterious shapes. Before the cloth was removed my brother would read the Christmas gospel. My part was to speak a poem to the child Jesus at the crib, and obviously between the two the old Christmas carols were sung.

Christmas was the most important family festival of the year—but at the same time it was firmly grounded in the church's Christmas liturgy: before the household gathering, the whole family had been at Midnight Mass.

For me, the church year with its feasts and festal seasons, its customs and remembrances of the biblical stories, was simply a matter of course. I grew into Christianity, in my case Roman Catholic Christianity, as I did into the pants and jackets my mother sewed for me. I should, of course, explain what I mean by "growing into" it. My parents were simple people. They struggled to get by with little money, and none of it was spent on fruit, vegetables, salad, or herbs for cooking. Those came from our own garden. My father even resoled our shoes in his basement workshop and regularly cut our hair in the living room. Our mother sewed nearly all the clothing for us four children, always a little larger than necessary, so that we could "grow into" it.

Later I learned that the same was true of baptism. In it the baptizand is given everything: the love of God the Father, the hidden life in Christ, the sheltering community of the church. All of that is symbolized by the white baptismal garment that is spread over the baby. Throughout her or his life the baptizand must grow into all that, including the adventure of faith.

To bring those great words down to earth a little I should say that my parents' faith was not naïve, simply received, or a habit of belief owed only to their Catholic milieu. My mother had two brothers who, in the liberal air of the city of Frankfurt am Main, had more or less lost their faith. She was exposed to their banter, sometimes even their ridicule. She had to decide for herself about her faith and the shape of her life in it.

The same was true for my father. He, indeed, came from a Catholic village in the Rhone district, but he ended up in Frankfurt, and before he became a locomotive engineer he worked on a major reconstruction of the federal railways. It was a "red" environment, and anyone who was known to attend church was ridiculed. One morning, when my father got to work, he found the others had built a little altar for him, with burning candles.

Likewise, the *church* environment in Frankfurt was not ordinary. We belonged properly to the parish of St. Gall, whose bounds mainly encompassed a thoroughly industrialized area in which the machine tools of the immense Adler plants hummed day and night. In Frankfurt people called this western industrial district "Cameroon," because the houses there were blackened by locomotive smoke and the countless chimneys of the factories. St. Gall was a workers' parish with a priest who was a genuine pastor. His name was Albert Perabo. It was there, after the war's destruction, that we found a tiny apartment in the middle of this "St. Gall quarter," close to the old parish church, which had also been bombed out.

Before that we had lived in the "Cowpasture Estate,"[2] built by the famous architect Ernst Georg Mai (1886–1970) on the principles of the garden-city movement. Since this settlement of railway workers was separated from the parish church to which we belonged by a railway freight station with a network of tracks a kilometer wide, we usually went to church at St. Elizabeth's in the Bockenheim district. It was much easier to get to. There, too, we found remarkably good priests. When it was time for the then-common annual "mission" the pastor did not call on the Capuchins, who put great stress on heaven and hell among other things, but sought out the Benedictines, who introduced us through the

[2] Kuhwaldsiedlung.

week to the liturgy of Holy Mass—which at that time, in the beginnings of the Liturgical Movement, was something entirely new.

That was the Catholic "biotope" in which I grew up: a consciously believing milieu that had to assert itself within a long-since liberal city that in many respects had forgotten God; a Christian milieu exposed to the chicanery of the Nazis (I will return to that); a Catholic living space that was thoroughly ecumenical in its outlook. All of it was pure grace!

It was only much later that I realized how little to be taken for granted my Christian socialization was at the time. For many of my later associates who grew up in the Westerwald mountains or in villages in Lower Franconia it was all quite different. *We* had to confess our faith. When we walked the long streets to worship on Sundays we proudly carried our hymnals in our hands. Everyone who met us could see that on Sunday morning we were not going just anywhere; we were on our way to church. Today a simple demonstration of that kind is no longer very common: the hymnals are not at home; they are in a big box behind the last pew in the church, to make it easy for the faithful. Why should they have to bring their own hymnals with them to church?

One other thing I need to say at this point is that already at the age of seven, exactly like my two older siblings, I was a bookworm. I read everything I could get my fingers on, the most exciting books sometimes over and over again. Often I would get to the end of a book and immediately start over from the beginning.

My mother knew that, of course. She saw to it—and this was not an easy thing in the Nazi era—that we always had books that, if possible, reflected a Christian environment, and whose "heroes" and "heroines" were often young people who consciously lived their faith. I owe a great deal to those books in that phase of my life, and I am still grateful to my mother for her vigilance. Once, many years later, she admitted to me that she herself read most of what I read, so that she would know what was influencing me at any time. How she managed it, what with her sewing and the work of raising four children, I still cannot comprehend. Certainly a lot of night hours must have been involved.

Here something else needs to be said: I did not grow up in a "holy family" where nothing was heard but the soft voices of the angels. In our family, just as in others, there were conflicts and quarrels between the siblings. Certainly our parents did not argue in our presence, but later I understood that between them, too, there were sometimes profound misunderstandings. Still, the conflicts concealed from us always ended in reconciliation, and there was between the two of them a quiet fidelity and matter-of-fact being-for-each-other that was rooted in their common faith.

2

School Days

Why do I believe in God? The second answer is: because I had not only my family but also the good fortune always to meet faithful Christians at the right moment. It began already with my friends who lived in the same neighborhood, who played hide-and-seek with me on the borders of the gigantic freight yard, and with whom I made my First Communion.

That took place in 1942. Under National Socialist rules all religious events had to be restricted to church spaces. But, as I have said, we were fairly far removed from St. Gall, the center of our assigned parish. So a family of believers who lived in our neighborhood made their basement available for First Communion instruction as needed, and created a special, cozy room for it. One of the assistant priests came there every week to teach the candidates, and it was impressed on the children involved that "on no account may the lot of you all arrive at the same time." So we chose slightly different times, and we did not play in front of the house in question but went directly through the door, which was open only a crack. Some came through the garden door behind the house. Only our parents knew how risky it all was. We ourselves saw it as a kind of Wild West drama between hostile tribes, a game of creeping around and hiding out.

My luck in always having faithful Christians around me at the right moment continued with the assistant priests who at that time were assigned to every city parish. My mother invited one or another of them to coffee or supper from time to time. It was important for my parents because they could hear from the lips of the invited clergy what the wiser Roman Catholics thought about Hitler and National Socialism. We children were not allowed to be present at those conversations, but obviously that made us aware that we were not supposed to know anything about them. Once, as the adults' discussion became more excited, I heard through the closed door that they were constantly talking about a "criminal," and I knew who it was: Adolf Hitler.

Obviously we also understood how much our parents respected and valued their clergy. I never heard from either of them a single negative word about priests or bishops. Besides, there was no reason why there should have been such: the clergy we knew were polite, reserved, and lovable people.

The sermons of one of these assisting priests were regularly monitored by an informant for the Gestapo (the *Geheimstaatspolizei* = "State Secret Police"). He sat in one of the last pews, paid close attention, and wrote down what was said. Obviously the priest in question avoided naming the Nazis' crimes directly: that would have brought him straight to the concentration camp at Dachau (where ultimately 2,720 European clergy were imprisoned, 447 of them from Germany and Austria. Many Polish priests were especially singled out to be murdered there and a total of 94 German and Austrian clergy met their deaths in Dachau).

But to get back to our assistant priest: he was very clever. For example, he preached at length on the Fifth Commandment, "You shall not kill," and explained that here the Bible was speaking of the killing of the innocent. The congregation, of course, knew precisely what he meant by that and which criminals he had in mind. So did the Gestapo. So it happened that he was hauled into the Gestapo's interrogation rooms any number of times: there he was questioned and threatened. However, I knew nothing of those events at the time; I only learned of them after the war. What I did experience directly was the following:

The elementary school (then called a "Volksschule" or "public school") to which our parents sent us had originally been a Catholic school, as was obvious from its name: "St. Boniface." After Hitler's seizure of power its ties to the church were quickly severed. Teachers who were not members of the National Socialist

German Workers' Party or did not toe the line were sent to country places in the flatlands or were barred from teaching; they were replaced in the St. Boniface school by Nazis faithful to the Party. These imposed their Party ideology in nearly every subject—writing, reading, arithmetic, homework. One key element of this was that we had to memorize Hitler's biography and be able to recite it over and over again:

> Our leader Adolf Hitler was born on the 20th of April of the year 1889 in Braunau am Inn. Even as a very young child . . . etc.

I could never recite the long text correctly when I was called on by our teacher, and that happened regularly. As punishment I had to stand in front of the class and hold out my left hand; the teacher would strike my fingertips violently with a long ruler. Worse than the pain was the social ostracism that accompanied it. I often woke bathed in sweat from nightmares about it. I did not dare tell my parents anything about all this; they were only surprised at my miserable grades.

However, this traumatic nightmare had a good ending. Beginning in 1940, schools in German cities were gradually closed because of the ever-more-intensive English bombing raids. This gave the Nazis an excuse to deport not only schoolchildren but even younger ones out of the cities to National Socialist "homes" in the country, often far away in Eastern Germany (it was called "dispatching the children to the countryside"). Of course many parents were unwilling to cooperate and preferred to send their children to relatives who lived not so far away, in a village or small town. Our parents did so too, sending my brother, my older sister, and me to relatives in 1942: my brother to Limburg on the Lahn, my sister to the Rhön district, and me to Heppenheim in the Bergstrasse district in southern Hesse.

For me it was pure liberation. Suddenly I had a fair and friendly class teacher; it was a principle with him that Hitler's biography and other such stuff was not recited; I could again sleep peacefully at night, and my grades were presentable. The relatives under whose protection I lived were good, pious Christians. I felt as if I had been rescued, and I was simply happy. Those experiences also helped to shape my faith.

Still, my encounter with National Socialism had begun much earlier. That "meeting" was of a similar nature. Certainly I cannot remember it myself; I was too little. But people told me about it many times afterward.

At that time the Frankfurt airport was adjacent to the city: it was the airport "Am Rebstock" and it was close to the railroad workers' development I have described, where we lived at the time. When Hitler landed there it could happen that he would then be driven through our neighborhood to the nearby assembly hall, standing in a Mercedes convertible with his hand held high in the "German salute." Long lines of people stood along the streets on such occasions and shouted "Heil Hitler."

It happened once that my parents were part of the crowd and they held me up so that I could see the Führer. But, as I was told later, I did not look at him; instead, I studied the faces of the crowd pressing around us. Evidently I had never, in my previous childhood, seen women whose faces were so fanatically distorted as those around me then. I am told that I began to cry bitterly and buried my face in my mother's shoulder.

Now I need to say something about our religious education in the Nazi period. I already touched on the subject in speaking of our instruction for First Communion. The National Socialists had eliminated religious instruction from the schools, so it had to take place within the boundaries, and the buildings, of the parishes. Certainly that was not a bad thing: in this way the lessons became a genuine instruction in the faith.

School instruction did not resume in Frankfurt in 1945, immediately after the war's end: the schools were all in ruins. Therefore, as in the Nazi period, religious instruction continued within the several parishes. We called it "parish time." As a result, during the war years and especially in the immediate aftermath I received an unusually thorough instruction in religion from our assistant priests. We learned many parts of the catechism by heart—and I not only memorized them. The contents were carefully and rationally explained to us. The crucial thing, though, was that we all came of our own accord, and the background for the instruction was the common life of the church: we saw each other every week at Sunday Mass.

Obviously there was a great deal more to my socialization in the church. When I was eight, I became an altar boy. My brother Norbert, six years older than I, was not only a great model for me in everything but also a real helper. He taught me the Latin Mass prayers. Simply because I was an altar boy I went to Mass every Sunday, but often on weekdays as well. That was nothing special; it was a matter of course.

I cannot say that as a child or teenager I was gripped by the Mass. For me the eucharistic celebration was more like a game: being on time, giving the correct responses, and keeping the correct posture as an altar boy: no wobbly genuflections, no fidgeting, no mistakes.

Of course, worship was a kind of home to me: the colorful windows in the church of St. Elizabeth that slowly lost their hues in the course of evening devotions and were transformed into a mysterious dark red; the incense; the liturgical vestments; the solemn silence when the people were blessed with the monstrance; the soft light of the many candles; the hymns with their often-archaic German and their familiar melodies. With all that, something unquenchable must have sunk into my heart.

Sometimes I was even really able to pray after communion, when I had regained my seat and was holding my hands in front of my face, as was customary then; still, a great deal was simply a routine process. For a long time the homily was completely uninteresting to me. I didn't listen, but let my eyes roam. Even the so-called children's Masses scarcely changed anything.

Change only happened when I was seventeen or eighteen. The war was long since in the past. Then, slowly and still tentatively, my first real questions about faith arose. If I remember correctly it was primarily a matter of problems with church history. In high school history classes I was confronted for the first time with the dark side of Christianity's past: battles against heretics, persecution of Jews, schisms, wars of religion, hostility and even hatred between the confessions—the whole spectrum.

My own perspective was still wholly apologetic. I volunteered, in my primarily Lutheran high school class, to give a talk on the

Reformation in order to present the Catholic perspective. I wanted to know more about it, and I sought out special literature in the library—but only in order to defend the Catholic Church.

At the same time I also began to listen to the Sunday sermons; after all, I needed material with which to defend my own faith. But it soon appeared that the kind of sermons usually preached in the church were not of much use. They were insufficient. And it was precisely at that point that good luck found me again.

We were now back in the Cowpasture Estate, and our house was not very far from the University of Frankfurt—only about half an hour's walk. And near the university were the quarters of the Catholic Student Association, where the college chaplain Ottmar Dessauer, son of the famous scientist, entrepreneur, and publisher Friedrich Dessauer,[1] celebrated Mass every Sunday for the Catholic students. Now I went there on as many Sundays as I could, even though I was not a university student and still had two more years of high school ahead of me.

For me, Ottmar Dessauer was phenomenal. His sermons were worked out in detail. He read them from a manuscript, scarcely glancing at his audience, but that did not bother me at all since everything he said was reasonable, enlightening, and gave answers to precisely the questions that were wandering through my head at the time.

It was clear that Dessauer had a father for whom natural science and faith were not opposed and for whom it was a matter of course that Christian faith had a public character: it must be witnessed to. Ottmar Dessauer also lived in community with other well-known pastors in the Frankfurt Oratory of St. Philip Neri.

Very soon I was attending his Sunday Mass every week. From him I learned that the findings of modern natural science and the biblical account of creation do not contradict each other because they speak on completely different levels. I also learned from him

[1] Friedrich Dessauer (1881–1963) was a famous German physicist who focused on radiology. He was also an entrepreneur. More than that, he was a representative of the Center Party in the Reichstag, was hunted by the Nazis, and had to leave Germany. Still more, he was a publisher and co-owner of the *Rhein-Mainische Volkszeitung*. In short: he was one of the best-known Roman Catholics in the period between the two world wars.

that the ongoing evolution of organic life over endlessly long periods of time, with its trials and errors, ceaseless reproduction, mutation, and selection, springs from the one, unceasing creative act of God.

All that was so enlightening that even today I feel sorry for Christian fundamentalists who fight the idea of evolution. For me, the fantastic history of evolution—even with its dead ends and false starts—is a sign of the greatness of the Creator, but above all a sign of how fully God desires the creation to be free.

I also encountered for the first time in Ottmar Dessauer a preacher who really "interpreted" the Gospel, turning the text back and forth, positively kneading it. Thus the Mass became an intellectual adventure that I loved to attend and even looked forward to. Ottmar Dessauer came at just the right time for me. That, too, was grace.

Of course, at this point I properly should recall many other people I met and who helped and guided me. The best and most interesting of them were women and men who were deeply grounded in the life of the church. Because of them I was at first completely baffled by the endless criticism and bad-mouthing of the church that became so common from the 1960s onward.

3

Youth Movement

In Western civilization a normal part of life is that young people, in the course of puberty, break out of the "family enclosure." The family was necessary; it gave the growing child shelter and security. But at some point one has to leave it. Certainly that process of separation from one's own family has looked very different in every age, and it has not existed everywhere. In some cultures it is frowned on even today or is virtually imperceptible.[1] In Europe, at least in some periods, it was very stormy indeed. That, at any rate, is how it was in Germany with the so-called "youth movement." It played an important part in my life, which is why it has to have a place here.

In what follows, certainly, I must paint the phenomenon of the "youth movement" with a broad brush. It had its beginnings in the second half of the nineteenth century and then, before and after the First World War, it attracted more and more young people—whether it was rooted in sports clubs, political parties, or the churches.

The ideals of this youth movement, still seeking to define itself, were simplicity, naturalness, inner truthfulness, self-responsibility, self-development ("youth guides youth"), a longing for a separate,

[1] It is worthwhile in this context to read Sabine Kuegler, *Child of the Jungle: The True Story of a Girl Caught Between Two Worlds* (New York: Warner Books, 2005). Kuegler spent her childhood and youth among the young people of the previously unknown Fayu tribe in the jungles of Papua New Guinea.

untouchable world of young people, protest against bourgeois life, and distancing from the "stuffy world" of adults. To make those programmatic ideas a little clearer, I will quote from the first volume of the autobiography of philosopher Josef Pieper (1904–1997). During his school years he was a member of an abstinence club for youth in which, suddenly, everything changed:

> From one day to the next one in five of us learned to play the lute or guitar; we threw away our petty-bourgeois celluloid collars and the clip-on ties that go with them, and wore open-neck shirts or carters' smocks; we let our hair grow long, deliberately to annoy people; suddenly long trousers and waistcoats were taboo, and we could only smile patronizingly at the elegant canes with knobs of silver or ebony with which we had already begun, at the age of sixteen, to swagger around. Outside the town, literally by the sweat of our brows, we transformed a derelict baroque pavilion into a clubhouse where we held evening sing-alongs. We learned (from whom?) the old folk dances, rehearsed plays by Hans Sachs and Andreas Gryphius and performed them in the open air. But, above all, the time had come for us to "go a-wandering."[2]

In the Catholic Church in Germany there were three youth groups that played an outstanding role: developing in a number of stages beginning in 1913 there was the society of "Quickborn-Freunde," centered in Burg Rothenfels, on the eastern border of the Spessart mountains, high above the valley of the river Main. This youth group became an important basis for the work of Romano Guardini; it was through him that the Liturgical Movement achieved broad influence within the Roman Catholic Church.

The year 1919 marked the founding of an association of Roman Catholic students in academies and high schools; it was called "Neudeutschland" (New Germany). Its spiritual life was shaped by the Jesuits; later it expanded to include universities. One of its most important programmatic aims was "shaping a new life in Christ." The years after World War I also saw the founding of "Heliand," an association of Roman Catholic girls in high schools.

[2] Josef Pieper, *No One Could Have Known: An Autobiography, the Early Years, 1904–1945*, trans. Graham Harrison (San Francisco: Ignatius Press, 1987), 38.

Heliand ("Savior") was the title of a harmony of the gospels in Old High German.

The three groups I have mentioned (there were others as well) were firmly grounded in the church—and it was a church that felt itself young and full of promise. Romano Guardini shaped the saying: "The church awakens in souls." That was true not only of the youth movement but it was especially appropriate to it. The primarily Latin Mass was replaced by "community Masses" with "prayer leaders" who recited certain parts of the Mass in German while the priest prayed them in Latin. Now there were "youth Masses," "young people's sermons," "youth pilgrimages," many new songs and periodicals dedicated to young people.

I can name some of those papers. They came from a number of youth movement centers and their names betray the new sense of life: "The New Beginning," "The Awakening," "The Covenant," "Icebreakers," "The Falcon," "The German Volunteers," "Comradeship," "Michael," "The Campfire," "The White Knight," "The Path to the Kingdom [*Reich*]." The very popularity of the word "Kingdom" reveals the ambivalence and vagueness of young people's language at the time: it could refer to the "*Reich* of Christ," but also the "*Reich* of Youth," or almost certainly the "German Reich." Or all three meanings could be dubiously blended together.

The National Socialists were able to adopt any number of concepts and rituals from the youth movement, but they stained them to match their own ideology, usurped them for the "Hitler Youth," and, after their seizure of power in 1933, forbade the "movement types" further use of them.

As far as the Roman Catholic Church was concerned, the new rulers very quickly forbade any kind of public work by Catholic groups, ignoring the concordat that had been made with the Vatican. The churches were only allowed to hold meetings in their own spaces. How did the bishops react to that prohibition?

Particularly indicative is the story of the "Affirmation Day for Catholic Youth." Not long after World War I the bishops had chosen Trinity Sunday (the first Sunday after Pentecost) as a day for young people to renew their profession of faith. It was celebrated especially in the cathedrals and larger churches with a major program for youth, featuring processions and torchlight parades.

The Nazis hated those festivals and tried to stop them. For that reason they scheduled their "Reich sport festival" precisely on that Sunday. That was highly effective, because many young people sought or were forced to participate in the sport festival. So the bishops shifted the affirmation day for youth to the feast of Christ the King, which was introduced by Pope Pius XI in 1925. Thus the last Sunday in the church year became the great day of protest by Catholic youth. Confession of Jesus Christ, the king of the world, was deliberately set against the cult of Hitler. Newly created songs for Christ the King played an important role in those celebrations. Across the Atlantic a hymn by Daniel Lord, SJ, published in 1932 by *The Queen's Work* in St. Louis, Missouri, is a close parallel:

> An army of youth
> Flying the standards of truth,
> We're fighting for Christ, the Lord.
> Heads lifted high,
> Catholic Action our cry,
> And the Cross our only sword.
> On earth's battlefield
> Never a vantage we'll yield
> As dauntlessly on we swing.
> Comrades true, dare and do
> 'Neath the Queen's white and blue,
> For our flag, for our faith,
> For Christ the King.[3]

[3] The German song quoted here by the author, "Uns rufet die Stunde, uns dränget die Zeit . . ." (The hour summons us, the time urges us . . .) is from 1934, the music by Adolf Lohmann and text by Rev. Franz Morthorst. A battle hymn with a march-rhythm that seized the spirit of all who sang it, it was one of the most popular songs and was to be heard in ceremonies of religious profession and countless "song vigils." In the United States, where the Sodalities of the Blessed Virgin Mary flourished in the 1940s–1950s, Daniel Lord's hymn played a similar role, not as protest against the U.S. government but certainly in the context of the Cold War. I still know it by heart seven decades later; it was central to the annual Christ the King assemblies of Catholic youth in the Houston Colosseum during my high school years (1952–56).—Tr.

This, and similar marching songs for Catholic youth, were battle hymns in march rhythm, gripping all those who sang them. Certainly their language and musical form were things of their own time; it would be impossible to sing them now. Their "knightly" romanticism and military-mystical language would be unbearable. "No resting, no standing, storming the heights . . ." (or "On earth's battlefield never a vantage we'll yield, as dauntlessly on we swing . . ."). What did that mean? Public resistance to National Socialism? Hardly! The texts remained nobly vague. In Germany, though, in the years of the SS, the Gestapo, and the Hitler Youth, it was indeed clear to many young Catholics that these songs were opposed to the Nazi dictatorship. For example, when they spoke of "night and fog" they were referring to the mendacious NS-ideology. And Christ the king was the real ruler, not Adolf Hitler.[4]

Certainly we may be puzzled today by some of the words: for example, "youth" (*Jungvolk*). The Nazis called members of the Hitler Youth, ages ten to fourteen, "*Jungvolk.*" But that was another of the many terms they had stolen from the youth movement.

"Uns rufet die Stunde" was to be found in then-popular Catholic songbooks such as *The Grey Songboat*. It, together with the *Christmas Hymnal* and *Church Song*, and periodicals like "Michael" and "The Watch," were products of the work done in the youth center in Düsseldorf under the leadership of the youth pastor Ludwig Wolker and his helpers, including especially Georg Thurmair[5]—that is, until 1938 when the National Socialists abolished all non-state youth groups by decree. In 1939 a law was enacted requiring universal membership in the Hitler Youth.

But why am I telling you all this? After World War II, when we were finally done with the "Thousand-Year Reich," the classic youth movement bloomed again for a time. I completed school in the year 1954 at the Heinrich-von-Gagern Gymnasium in Frankfurt,

[4] See Wilhelm Schepping's essay, "Christ-Königslieder gegen Hitlers Regime," *Archiv für schlesische Kirchengeschichte* 71, ed. Rainer Bendel (Münster: Aschendorff, 2014), 281–316.

[5] For Georg Thurmair see the informative description in Elisabeth Thurmair, ed., *Ein Gast auf Erden: Georg Thurmair. Mahner, Rufer, Rebell* (Eggenfelden: Aventinus Verlag, 1986).

and it was precisely in those years between 1945 and 1954 that I was able to take part in what had once distinguished the Catholic youth movement. It was a late blooming—or, to put it better, a late summer of a remarkable time in the church. I can recall those years after the war in many vivid and unforgettable images.

One such arises especially often in my memory: at that time the Cathedral of St. Bartholomew rose high over the broad field of ruins that was the old city of Frankfurt. The tower was still standing, together with the bare walls of the burned-out nave. Next to the cathedral ruins, members of the Catholic Youth had built some of its stones into a tall, slightly sloping stage for the performances of their amateur theater group. There, on summer evenings, a great crowd of people gathered amidst the ruins and participated in those shows. I have forgotten the names of the plays, but not my avid listening and looking.

A second image: our curate at that time, Hermann-Josef Heyer, could be seen for several hours every morning, for months, wheeling away the ruins of the church of St. Gall. The only half-destroyed entrance hall of the church was to be rebuilt as a temporary sanctuary. Young people from the parish joined in spontaneously, later also in mixing mortar and even raising the walls. For us the whole was symbolic of the rebuilding of the church in Germany.

Still another picture (I am no longer clear about the year): every month, on a particular evening, crowds of young people streamed to the church of St. Bernard in the North End for "youth sermons." (The church seated eight hundred.) This monthly event was popular not only for the usually exciting sermon but also for the long pilgrimage through the city, there and back again. People went on foot in very diverse groups. The youth sermon in St. Bernard's was simply *the* social event that regularly brought Frankfurt's Catholic youth together.

The same is true of the annual "youth pilgrimage" to the Marienthal monastery in the Rheingau. As a matter of course we traveled the long road from Frankfurt to the Rheingau on bicycles and there, despite the clouds of gnats and mosquitoes, we pitched our tents in the meadows around the monastery. Here, as on so many other occasions, common faith was an integral aspect, along with sports.

It was similar with another big annual event of those years, the Corpus Christi procession. In our home parish of St. Gall that procession traveled mostly along the long, broad Frankenallee. Men, women, religious sisters, and of course the parish youth were each responsible for one of the four altars: that is to say, for *their* altar. Here competition came into play: which group had the most beautiful altar with the most greenery and the loveliest carpets of flowers? As far as we were concerned, it was always the youth group's altar. The evening before, it was usually the case that a rumor (maybe invented by one of us?) circulated that the Communists would try to destroy the altars during the night. So it was clear: the older youth had to guard the four altars. Weary but happy, they then participated the next morning in the solemn Corpus Christi Mass and the procession. I still have a photo of the huge number of young people marching behind their Christ-banners.

Of course I also belonged to a "youth group" with a "group leader," a pennant, weekly meetings, and jaunts through half of Germany. On those trips we often joyfully sang a traveling song from the 1930s:

> We have journeyed throughout all of Germany,
> From the sea to the alpine snows,
> The wind still plays through the hair of our heads,
> The wind of the mountains and seas.
>
> Our ears hear the roaring of rivers,
> The murmuring sound of the woods,
> The clang of the bells of cathedrals,
> The singing of larks in the fields.
>
> Our eyes are filled with the starlight,
> The shimmer of high-summer heat,
> And deep in our souls is the far-far-away,
> The longing that never is stilled.
>
> So we have journeyed through Germany,
> From the sea to the alpine snows,
> We still have new roads to travel
> And other new lands to behold.

At some point I then became a "group leader" myself and was entrusted with a number of boys ages nine to eleven. I remember a lot about that, too. On the one hand there were the weekly group meetings in the parish hall. I had to learn how to deal with a lively bunch of about ten boys, patiently but often also clearly and firmly.

Every summer we took the train to the Westerwald where the diocese had a tent camp in the valley of the River Gelb. Twelve big pyramidal American tents stood there, neatly arranged in two rows with the campfire between them, dominated by a great cross made of birch logs. There were morning and evening prayers in front of the cross, common meals in the open air, hikes, sports competitions, evening song circles, nightly scouting games, and a lot more. To get my tent of boys, still seething with excitement, to settle down at night I learned to tell made-up stories, as suspenseful as possible, when they were all bedded down in the dark. Often I reworked stories from books I had read. After a little while I made my voice softer and softer—and if no one protested I knew that all the boys had finally fallen asleep.

More powerful than the big tent camp, however, were little trips with my group to the Spessart Forest. There was a farm whose barn we could use for sleeping; the woman of the house cooked midday dinner and an evening meal for us, and between those we ranged through the woods. Often we sat in the evening, each of us wrapped in a blanket, high above a steep cliff; we sensed how darkness fell and the forest behind us became quieter and quieter. For me that was an opportunity to talk with the boys about all and sundry, including the church and faith. We finished with evening prayer in common.

Again: why am I writing about all this? At the time I could not have put it into words and probably did not even think much about it. Today it is clear to me that children and youth indeed have to experience the faith of their parents and be introduced to it by them: that forms the indispensable basis for their own belief. But at some point—and it can begin very early—they also have to experience Christian faith outside their own families, and not only from adults or older people but also from those of their own age and younger. The same was true, of course, for me. But here I need to give some examples.

In the youth group for which I was responsible there was a young boy who was very small and extremely shy. He was the youngest in the group and he was being raised by his grandmother because his parents ran a bakery and were tied to it half the night and all day long. Unfortunately, he was also nicknamed "Holdi."[6] Two children in his class used to tease him. It had happened any number of times that when school let out they told him: "You stand here under this tree and wait till we come back and tell you that you can go home." Holdi then waited obediently for hours, not daring to leave.

Someone in the youth group who was in Holdi's class brought up the subject, and then we said to Holdi: "If that happens again, wait till the two have gone and then just take off for home. If they give you any trouble, they'll have to deal with our whole group." I didn't know exactly what we would have done in that case; there were a number of possibilities. But when it did happen again the little boy simply went away, and he had no further difficulties with the two boys who had played games with him. They probably just wanted to see how far they could go. I myself was deeply moved by the trust Holdi put in me and the whole group. For the first time I sensed what trust is and what it demands of the one on whom it is bestowed.

Also important to me were those of my own age in the youth group of which I myself was a part. There were not just the long trips through half of Germany during which we became deeply acquainted with each other. The construction company of Philipp Holzmann had dredged out a rather large pocket of sand and gravel in the extensive Frankfurt municipal forest (*Stadtwald*). They left behind them a lake that was fed by clean groundwater. Romantic as we then were, we called it the "Blue Eye of the Desert," even though it was surrounded by pine forests. On hot summer evenings we bicycled to it, usually on the spur of the moment, without planning. We were sure to meet others of us there, alone or in a group. But the point was not just the fun of swimming. There was always something to talk about, advice to seek and give, things to discuss. What was so important was that

[6] A popular name for a puppy.—Tr.

we also met in the church on Sundays. We did not believe in isolation; people our own age played an important part as well.

It is true that for me the most important individuals in this period were older persons without whom the parish's youth work would have been unimaginable. For example, there was a former youth leader named Josef Wild who, like so many others, had been conscripted near the end of the war, at the age of seventeen. The parish was immensely grateful to him for his work in building up new youth groups immediately after the war. In the meantime he had married, and I visited him often to learn of his war experiences, borrow books from him, and observe closely the wise and loving way he and his wife were raising their little daughter.

In the same way I still think often of our pastoral assistant in St. Gall, Gertrud Koob. At that time parish services were not as institutionalized and regulated as they are today. Although she was still very young, our pastor (Albert Perabo, previously mentioned) had asked her whether she wanted to help, and she had immediately agreed. With her warmth and approachability she quickly became the soul of the congregation. She was in charge of all the girls' groups, but many other people came to her with their questions and problems, seeking her out in the tiny parish office. She was like a big sister to me. (My own older sister had been killed on November 21, 1944, together with more than sixty other schoolchildren, when a plane strafed the train station at Hünfeld.) We lent each other books and conversed about films such as *Nightwatch* or *The Song of Bernadette* or discussed holding a dance for the parish youth. The deep faith of Gertrud Koob was one of the many things that later helped me to become a priest.

I could go on and on about the faces and happenings of that time, but it must have become clear by now how indebted I am to the second flowering of the youth movement: the carefree companionship with older people, those of my own age, and younger children as well. It was a profoundly important time for me: the experience of community in faith outside my parental home.

4

Decisions

Nearly everything I have said about myself thus far amounts to what sociologists call a "gentle socialization." In our context it means that I grew up, unresistingly, in the basic forms of the faith. I never made any real decisions: others modeled faith for me, explained it to me, pointed me to the right questions, and showed me how one can live as a Christian.

And I *wanted* faith, as one *wants* to eat a hearty slice of bread. Still, the statement that "others 'modeled' faith for me" is somewhat problematic. They did not deliberately "model" something for me; they simply lived their faith.

Here again I can give an example: my father always prepared very deliberately for his work as a locomotive engineer. The carbide lamp[1] was carefully maintained; the schedules, especially those with the current "slow stretches," were studied again; one or several packages of food for meal breaks were assembled and then stowed together with other necessities. On long trips—for example, from Frankfurt to Leipzig—my father had to spend the night in railroad lodgings. One day, in search of something, I rushed without knocking into my parents' bedroom just before my father was

[1] Carbide lamps were used by the German railways, and elsewhere, until the end of the 1970s. Such lamps were made up of two connected vessels: the upper container dripped water into the lower one, which was filled with calcium carbide. This produced a gas that was conveyed to a burner, where it glowed with a bright flame that was situated in front of a mirror. Those carbide lamps had to be tended very carefully.

about to go to work. He was kneeling there on the floor, his arms resting on the bed, and praying—obviously for an accident-free trip. I suddenly realized, at a stroke, that he evidently did that every time before going to work, but always behind closed doors. I retreated from the room, almost frightened. This was not an act of "modeling." It was simply living faith. I will never forget that image of my father at prayer.

"Gentle socialization in faith": at that time I did not experience any struggles with faith, any crises, any gradual erosion. Mine was an organically matured and still unshaken faith. I did not experience a crisis of faith even when, at the age of eighteen, I fell seriously ill with hepatitis and for nearly six months had to drag myself around day by day, exhausted and dead tired. After all, I had learned that God can test us, bring us into detours, lay burdens on our shoulders—that is all part of a Christian life. I simply accepted my illness. I did not pose bitter questions to God and I certainly did not make accusations. Mine was a rather sheltered and unchallenged faith. Of course, that was not enough in the long run. Something more had to happen.

When I was twenty-one and had already completed two semesters of German and Latin studies (my ambition was to be a high school teacher) I was suddenly faced with the question whether God had called me to the priesthood. The external impulse did not come from my parents, who had never spoken to me on that subject, nor did it come from my brother, who had already entered the Jesuit order. Instead, I received it from a Jesuit professor named Heinrich Bacht (1910–1986), whom I greatly respected for his humor and his willingness to help. One day when I was visiting him he asked me about my possible calling to be a priest. I disagreed strongly—and at the same time I was deeply moved. As I left him I knew that I was being faced with a decision that would affect my whole life. Now it was a direct challenge about the role of God in my life, and it was something whose startling force was completely new to me.

The decision was made within a few days, or more precisely within a few hours. I repeatedly imagined both possibilities: what I had dreamed of in bright fantasies and what was suddenly before me: a completely different life that would be directly and solely about service to the Gospel.

I still remember exactly what was decisive in the midst of these ponderings and thoughts, the twistings and searchings for ways of escape. First came the insight that the situation into which I had suddenly fallen—and that confronted me, so naked and unprotected, with God—could come only from God and must be about "God's will." A second thought arose again and again: when your life is at an end and, in death, you ultimately stand before God, what would be better—having chosen for God or for your own sweet dreams about life?

It was probably, once again, pure grace that I could make a decision so swiftly then. As soon as I had clearly chosen to be a cleric—more precisely, a pastor—I was filled with a profound peace and quiet joy. It was an experience of God: I have been absolutely certain of that ever since. No one can convince me otherwise.

As a matter of fact, this experience was repeated in similar fashion on a number of occasions. There were further decisions that profoundly changed my life; I will give an account of them in due course. What happened then, certainly, was a fundamental choice; everything that came later was built on it. In retrospect this fundamental decision showed me that a received faith in which one has simply grown up cannot suffice in the long run—especially not in our time when the majority of those we encounter every day no longer believe in God.

As Christians we are living in a time that has long since ceased to be that of a sunsetting youth movement or of the national "people's" church. For years now we have found ourselves in a situation like what is constantly depicted in the Bible and was familiar to the early church: we can no longer avoid choosing between "yes" to the one, holy God, to serve the one who leads us into freedom, or assenting to an unreflective, often matter-of-course "yes" to the many "gods of society" who seek without ceasing to broaden their spheres of power.[2]

[2] When I speak in this book, here and elsewhere, of the "gods of society" or "gods of this world," obviously I do not intend a total rejection of the society in which we live. That would be absurd. What I mean is that the gods that were worshiped in antiquity—and that obviously continue to exist—are "powers" of this world. Ultimately they are models that may be good and helpful, but can also be catastrophic. Think only of Nazism or the newly growing anti-Judaism, or simply of the hatred, seductions, and demonizations that pervade the social

From among the many biblical texts that speak about this moment of decision let me select two that are especially striking: first, Joshua 24:14-15. Israel has entered the Promised Land, but it is by no means empty of people. It is already occupied—by many gods and powers, deeply entrenched pagan principles, and the often-inhuman rituals of Canaan. Israel, after its time in the wilderness, is now again living within the sphere of gods that are part of the "blood and soil" of every land—and the longer Israel lives in the "Land" the more it accommodates to its surroundings. It takes part in the rituals and the world of gods belonging to Canaan.

That is how the Bible tells it, and that is how it may well have been in history also. The gods of the lands were attractive: otherwise Israel would not have repeatedly fallen for them. They were as enticing as unbounded sexuality is today, together with deliberately produced exhilaration, nature mysticism, misuse of power, violence, and the painfully anxious safeguarding of all the necessities of life.

But back to the Bible! There the twenty-fourth chapter of the book of Joshua marks a decisive point. Shortly before his death the military leader Joshua summons all the tribes of Israel at Shechem and demands a clear choice. The people are to decide whom they will serve: the God who led them out of the old society, out of unfreedom and slavery—that is, the God who makes history and, as "creator of heaven and earth," is not bound to any land—or the gods tied to their own lands, who demand the same old fear of demons, service to idols, and unfreedom. The decision is to be made freely. The people must "choose" (Josh 24:15, 22)—for or against YHWH—but one thing they cannot do: try to serve YHWH *alongside* the gods of the land. So Joshua says to the assembled people:

> Put away the gods that your ancestors served beyond the River [Euphrates] and in Egypt and serve the LORD. Now if you are unwilling to serve the LORD, choose this day whom you will serve, whether the gods your ancestors served in the

media today. Too many young people are delivered up to them, with no power to resist.

> region beyond the River or the gods of the Amorites in whose land you are [now] living, but as for me and my household, we will serve the LORD. (Josh 24:14-15)

As I have already said: the demand for clear and unequivocal decision runs through the whole Bible. The same basic structure of faith is visible in John's Gospel. In his long speech at Capernaum, Jesus reveals himself as the "bread of life" (John 6:35, 48). The absoluteness of his language evokes a decision among his listeners, even including his disciples. The text specifically emphasizes that Jesus' disciples were among those who "complained" at what he said. The effect was thus precisely the same as in Israel's journey through the wilderness: as they had then "complained" against Moses when their resistance was, in fact, against God (Exod 16:6-8), so now they complain against Jesus—and that resistance is directed at God. Then comes the result: "many of his disciples turned back and no longer went about with him" (John 6:66).

Then Jesus turns to the Twelve, the core of his eschatological gathering of the people of God. He grants full freedom even to this group he has chosen. He says: "Do you also wish to go away?" Jesus speaks of "going away." That is important. It is not simply a matter of agreeing with a mere teaching, an abstract choice between theological theories or even "strategic" questions about proclamation. It is about coming to and remaining with Jesus. The disciples have to set their whole lives in motion. If they *come* to Jesus, they come to faith, and if they *go away* from him, they lose their faith.

So it is in this sense that Jesus asks the Twelve: "Do you also wish to go away?" (John 6:67). He would rather start over than continue with disciples whose half-heartedness will bring down the work of God. It is better if only a few remain and show, by their faith and companionship, what this new thing looks like. And as once Joshua had done, so now Simon Peter paves the way for the others, steps forward, and says:

> Lord, to whom can we go? You have the words of eternal life. We have come to believe and know that you are the Holy One of God. (John 6:68-69)

At present, as then, the church is living in a situation in which many are becoming skeptical, gradually letting their received faith wither or else turning away from the church in disgust. But when they do that they turn away from Jesus, even if in the moment they may not really wish to do so.

This situation demands today that every Christian reconsider her or his own position: "What do I want to do with my life? Whom will I serve? The gods of society or the true God? Myself or Jesus and his cause? Hopeless gossamer clouds of dreams or what God has planned for creation?" Each must decide.

However, at the same time we must consider this: as important and irreplaceable as this fundamental decision is, it can look very different, depending on the circumstances. We are not always standing with Israel at Sinai or with the twelve tribes and Joshua in Shechem. There are also the many little decisions, altogether unremarkable in appearance, that may still concentrate gradually in a basic choice: not holding a grudge against someone who has wounded us, helping someone in need, consoling someone who is sorrowing, contradicting someone who is ridiculing the church—there are countless steps that seem trivial but that can become a path, and ultimately a road.

Probably, in the hour when we ultimately stand before Christ and have arrived completely in the presence of God, we will be astonished to see that the great decisions of our lives were fed by infinitely many little daily choices—and even by the help and hopes of those who have lovingly and faithfully accompanied us through our lives.

5

Philosophy

Thus the decision was made. I wanted to join the clergy—more precisely, to be a priest and then a pastor in my home diocese of Limburg. I abandoned my Latin studies without a tear, but giving up German studies was really hard. Old High German and Middle High German had sounded in my ears like a marvelous invitation. I had read some poems by Walter von der Vogelweide so often that I could recite them by heart. I had also acquired some professional literature, especially editions of the classics. For example, I had read nearly all of Heinrich von Kleist's stories and dramas, as well as most of the works of Thomas Mann—including his diaries and *Doctor Faustus*. Only the tetralogy *Joseph and His Brothers* was still unattempted.

So now I was "majoring in" theology—in my home city, Frankfurt, at the Philosophisch-Theologische Hochschule Sankt Georgen. There I was not only to complete four semesters of philosophy; I also found most excellent teachers. In those two years I heard lectures on philosophical aspects of psychology, philosophical questions arising out of current physics, philosophical ethics, epistemology (theories of what knowledge really *is*), and above all philosophical doctrines of God. Even today I still draw on this long, basic introduction to philosophical thinking.

For indeed, what was offered us by the Jesuits in Sankt Georgen was not just the history of philosophy, as necessary as that is. It was a systematic investigation of the most important basic concepts of philosophy, and still more: an introduction to philosophical thinking as such. I can still picture two of my professors at that time: Helmut Ogiermann[1] and Caspar Nink.[2] They did not simply teach. No, each of them could enter into a thought process during lectures in which he simply forgot about his listeners and only pursued the subject at hand.

For example, Professor Ogiermann might speak about proofs of the existence of God, but it was not just a matter of "proofs." Ultimately it was the implacable question: "Why is there something and not nothing?" Thomas Aquinas had posed the same question, and Martin Heidegger formulated it later anew.[3] Helmut Ogiermann asked it, too, now in front of *us*, as if he was being confronted by it for the first time—and, besides, as the ultimate and most important of all questions.

To this day neither Immanuel Kant's epistemological objections nor the eternal back-and-forth about the possibility of proving God's existence have been able to tear me away from the stunning impact of that one question: "Why is there a world, a universe, being itself, and not, instead, an absolute, eternal nothingness?"

One may, of course, ask why theology needs philosophy, and why candidates for the priesthood must first study philosophy. The basic answer is very simple: Christian faith is not opposed to reason; it strives for it. It tries to imbue all truths of faith with our God-given reason. As Pope Francis has written in his apostolic exhortation *Evangelii Gaudium* (The Joy of the Gospel): "Faith is not fearful of reason; on the contrary, it seeks and trusts reason, since 'the light of reason and the light of faith both come from

[1] Father Helmut Ogiermann, SJ (1910–1995) was ordained priest in Berlin in 1939 and received his doctorate in philosophy at the Gregorian University in Rome in 1947. From 1952 to 1978 he was professor of philosophy at Sankt Georgen. He published his thoughts on the doctrine of God in his book, *Es ist ein Gott. Zur religionsphilosophischen Grundfrage* (Munich: J. Berchman, 1981).

[2] Father Caspar Nink (1885–1975) was ordained priest in 1917 and received his doctorate under Edmund Husserl in Freiburg in 1924. He was professor of philosophy at Sankt Georgen from 1926 to 1953, and continued thereafter to lecture at the college.

[3] Cf. Martin Heidegger, *Was ist Metaphysik?* (Frankfurt: Klostermann, 1955). See now *Basic Writings: Martin Heidegger*, ed. David Farrell Krell, Routledge Classics (London: Routledge, 2010), 89–110.

God.' "[4] Concretely that means that before we occupy ourselves with the truths of faith as such we must first take into view the whole *preliminary* of faith: the human being, the soul, the spirit, knowledge, freedom, the world, the universe.

We are now living in a time in which the natural sciences and their technical applications are celebrating triumphs. We experience it tangibly in biology, medicine, communications, astronomy, and many other fields. These unfathomable successes of the natural sciences rest on a radical "reduction." What does that mean?

According to a famous saying of Galileo Galilei, natural science measures everything that can be measured, and beyond that it tries to make everything immeasurable into something measurable. That is, it is constantly expanding the sphere of the measurable, and that measuring and making-measurable leads to extraordinary discoveries. At the same time, however, it narrows our field of vision. Only a particular dimension of the world and reality can be understood in quantifiable terms through the reductionism of research. Still, the gigantic successes of this methodological reduction all too often mislead us into supposing that what we study with these methods is everything, the whole of reality—in other words, that what opens itself to our eyes as trained by the natural sciences is simply the whole world.

Obviously serious natural scientists do not fall victim to that deceptive conclusion. They know the limits of their methods. They are aware that every science has its own way of looking at things and its own methods, but as a result it also has its specific limits. They hold themselves to those limits and do not go beyond their own abilities in reaching their conclusions.

Regrettably, however, that is not the case with all natural scientists. A methodological self-limitation that is correct and appropriate is transformed by many into a *theory of the world* that asserts: "Nothing exists but what one can count, measure, and in some way make audible and visible." In a thus-reduced world, of course, God cannot exist—but neither is there any place for a great many

[4] *Evangelii Gaudium* 242, quoting Thomas Aquinas, *Summa contra Gentiles* I, 7; cf. John Paul II, Encyclical Letter *Fides et Ratio* (14 September 1998), 43: AAS 91 (1999), 39.

other things such as soul, spirit, person, freedom, and love in their proper senses. All of that is degraded to mere projections corresponding to no reality.

Our studies in philosophy at Sankt Georgen in Frankfurt included many discussions of scientific method. We were repeatedly shown how crucial *clarity of method* is for all sciences—the natural sciences as well as the sciences of history, philosophy, and theology. And because so much depends on it—today more than ever—I want at this point to introduce a concrete example to illustrate the subject of methodological clarity. It is directly connected to the God question that is the subject of this book. What I am about to say also sheds light on the clear and intuitively accessible way that philosophy was pursued at Sankt Georgen. As an illustration I have chosen one of the most famous paintings of the twentieth century: Pablo Picasso's *Guernica*.[5]

There is much in this image that a natural scientist could investigate: for example, by measuring the frame on which the canvas is stretched, and then the canvas itself. Its dimensions are 3.39 meters by 7.77 meters,[6] a surface area of 26.34 square meters. The wood of the frame could be studied by radiocarbon methods to determine its age; the woven structure of the canvas could be analyzed, as well as the chemical composition of the colors and the nature of their distribution on the surface. The oil paints used could be subjected to pigment analysis in order to determine whether there are any secondary overpaintings. Above all, the examination would tell us that today the fabric of this gigantic painting by Picasso is in extremely fragile condition. That would not be simply nothing. Natural-scientific methods could say a great deal about the material substratum of the painting—but nothing more than that.

An historian could reveal more: for example, by informing us that in 1936 Pablo Picasso had been commissioned by the then-

[5] Readers who want to view the painting while reading this section can easily locate it on Wikipedia by searching "Guernica (Picasso)."

[6] Approximately 11 feet high and 25.6 feet wide, some 280 square feet.

government of Spain to paint a picture for the Spanish pavilion in the 1937 World Exhibition in Paris. At first he considered the motif of "the painter and the painter's model," but on April 26, 1937, fighter aircraft from the German Condor Legion, in league with Francisco Franco, bombarded the Basque city of Guernica. This was the first large-scale bombing ever carried out against a city, and its deliberate intent was to destroy the city and its inhabitants. Picasso chose that horrifying event as the subject of his picture. After the end of the exhibition his much-discussed painting entered on a long journey through Northern Europe and eventually to the United States, where from 1939 to 1981 it hung in the Museum of Modern Art in New York. Later it was returned to Spain, and since 1992 it has been in the Museo Reina Sofia in Madrid. So we know quite a bit about the history of the painting, its origin, its travels through part of the world, and its ultimate location. Even so, we still know almost nothing about the picture itself and how Picasso dealt with his subject.

So we now need the work of art historians, who can apply their own methods to the painting. They would, at last, reveal more about the image itself: for example, they would show us that the huge canvas surface is divided into three parts, a wide center panel and two narrower side panels, left and right—undoubtedly an echo of medieval winged altarpieces. The art historians would also show us that motifs from Christian depictions of the Passion are visible: twisted hands echo details from Matthias Grünewald's Isenheim altar, and the mother with her child on the left side reminds us of the *Pietà*. They would explain why Picasso did not use colors for this picture, but painted in *grisaille*. The reason was that the first floor of the Spanish pavilion featured a long series of black-and-white photos, and Picasso wanted to make a graphic connection to those. Above all, however, he wanted to draw viewers into the dark basement vaults where people sought refuge from the bombs: our eyes are led to the tiny cellar windows on the right and to the electric lamp at the upper border of the center portion that, like the eye of God, looks down on the whole. Art historians would also explain to us, however, what the bull dominating the left side signified for Picasso, and likewise the dying mare in the center. Those explanations would be enormously helpful;

they would at last bring us closer to what constitutes this picture *as a picture*.

But would a pure examination of the composition and its individual elements in terms of art history suffice? Surely not! How would we *understand* the picture—and by "understand" here I mean capture, grasp, comprehend at depth? It could happen, if we were to sit for a long time before Picasso's *Guernica*, if we discovered that the scene is filled with screaming mouths, and that the many individual parts of the image that at first present themselves separately are in fact a *fabric* of dismembered body parts. It could be that then, in light of this picture, we would absorb the full lunacy of war and violence.

What do I mean by all that? Picasso's world-famous painting cannot be comprehended by using natural-historical techniques or purely historical methods. It is, of course, altogether material, up to and including the light waves that touch our eyes and the impulses that reach our brains. And without its material substance the painting would be—nothing! It would simply not exist. But it is, on the basis of its material substratum, a *reality of unique quality*, something unreachable by natural-historical methods—as is also the case with other realities such as mind, soul, spirit, goodness, love, freedom, guilt, and violence. Grasping realities of that kind is the goal not only of an appropriate view of art; it is also the aim of a rational philosophy that is open to the multi-dimensionality of the world. Those were the realities that were the object of my philosophy studies in Frankfurt.

Only much later did I come to understand the degree to which philosophy at Sankt Georgen had led me not only to a rational faith but also to a rational way of proclaiming it. In fact, the dispute with a self-absolutizing natural science that insists it can, simply by using its own methods, offer a complete explanation of the world continued throughout my life. For example, there was the offensive atheism presented by Richard Dawkins's book, *The God Delusion*.

Toward the end of the twentieth century, brain researchers engaged in extensive and ever-new investigations of free will. Their intention was to demonstrate the impossibility of free will, based on organic processes in the brain (whose existence, of course, I do not contest). At that time, when such investigations were the subject of broad media coverage, I tried to put the comedy of those border violations into words:[7]

Now Let Us Be Consistent

> *"I want to write something about freedom of the will."* — *Nonsense! I ought to say: "A potential readiness has emerged within me that leads me to write about freedom of the will. I falsely label this neuronal event as deliberately brought about by myself." But even that admission is imprecisely formulated. There is no "I." After all, who has ever been able to demonstrate the existence of an "I" by means of physical experimentation? The illusion of the "I" belongs to the broad field of neuronal mechanisms of attribution. Therefore a correct formulation would be: "A potential readiness has built up within the collection of cells that constantly produces the illusion of an 'I' that compels that group of cells to write about freedom of the will."—That is crystal clear, is it not?*

Still, what is comical about the work of the brain specialists who are determined to prove that free will is an illusion lies elsewhere. They endlessly and urgently promote their deterministic view of reality. They want to convince us. They want their point of view about humanity to triumph. But they assume throughout that there *is* freedom of the human will, freedom in society. If there were not, they would have no need to propagandize for their position. If their theory of determinism were correct, what they consider "truth" would either prevail or it would not. They themselves cannot change that in the slightest. Why are they so ardently determined to spread their view of reality?

More than that—the inconsistency of these brain researchers goes much farther. If they love a spouse, then to be consistent they would not love a human being who has been *freely* attracted to them, but ultimately a highly developed humanoid robot. They themselves would scarcely want that to be the case—and the spouse most certainly would not!

[7] This text is taken from Gerhard Lohfink, *Heute – wann sonst? Unangepasstes über Gott und die Welt* (Stuttgart: KBW, 2nd ed. 2014), 72–73.

But enough with the excursus, and back to my studies in philosophy! Toward the end of the fourth semester I wrote my thesis on the concept of time in the works of Hedwig Conrad-Martius,[8] philosopher and student of Edmund Husserl. That project first made it clear to me how complex and profound—and also how relative—"time" is. Above all I understood (for the first *time*!) that it is methodologically impermissible to directly apply our concept of time, which is valid for our empirical space-time experience, to our future existence with God.

To say it as radically as possible: we must not assert that the dead "wait" with God for the end of the world, the resurrection of the dead, the world's judgment. Those who think about the "last things" of humanity presuppose that in our existence with God—as in our present existence—there is "ongoing" time: yesterday, today, tomorrow. But in our existence after death there can only be a combined, collected time fulfilled in God and no time "going on" in weeks, months, and years. Everything we say about our "time" with God is analogous. That is: the dissimilarity from our earthly experience of time is unimaginably greater than the similarity.

In order to express this radical dissimilarity in some approachable way we have to say nothing less than that we will rise "together" with all those who have already died—in fact, "together with Christ"—and in our own death we will already have "arrived" at the end of the world and the resurrection of all the dead. That is: we are all living, even now, in the immediate presence of the last things. Resurrection and final judgment are right in front of us, and the *now* that we still have is infinitely weighty. This gift of "today" compels us to join in the healing and sanctification of the world.

Of course, my philosophical thesis was only a first step in such reflections, but they have never left me, and they have shown me

[8] Hedwig Conrad-Martius (1888–1966) was a student of Edmund Husserl, the founder of phenomenology. Her book, *Die Zeit*, was published by Kösel in Munich in 1954. Edith Stein was one of her close friends.

how right and consequential biblical language about imminent eschatological expectation is. The great ideas and powerful images in the biblical tradition are all correct. Nothing needs to be discarded. We must only interpret them appropriately if we are to comprehend their depth. I later developed these initial insights into the *analogical* and not *univocal* concept of the last things for humanity in several books, especially *Is This All There Is? On Resurrection and Eternal Life*.[9]

[9] English translation by Linda M. Maloney (Collegeville, MN: Liturgical Press, 2017). Original: Gerhard Lohfink, *Am Ende das Nichts? Über Auferstehung und ewiges Leben* (Freiburg: Herder, 2017; 8th ed. 2022).

6

Intermission

It had long been the custom that candidates for the priesthood in the Diocese of Limburg, after completing their studies in philosophy, should spend their first two semesters of theological studies not in Frankfurt/Sankt Georgen but in the theology department of a university. I and my classmates went to Munich for a year. There we lived in a dormitory for theology students right next to the English Garden, a house directed by the Franciscan Sisters of Maria Stern,[1] who took the very best care of us.

We could freely choose which lectures we wanted to hear, but we were required to sit semester examinations for a certain number of *theology* courses. Beyond the purely subject-bound lectures I heard Romano Guardini, who spoke in the Auditorium Maximum for listeners from all faculties. I also regularly attended a course on "Psychiatry and Medical Symptoms," a world about which I knew almost nothing. But as a future pastor I wanted to learn as much as I could about suffering and the spiritual compulsions with which many people have to live. I have to admit that what attracted me most to this course was also that the interviews the different professors conducted, each time with a single sufferer and before a full auditorium, were extremely lively and fascinating.

Most important for me among the purely theological lectures were those of Josef Schmid (1893–1975) on the New Testament.

[1] Their community was founded in Augsburg in 1258.

I did not miss even one of them; I bought a Greek synopsis that I marked with colored pencils at the points where Matthew and Luke deviated from their Markan model and tried to discover the reasons for each. I also marked all the texts in which Matthew and Luke agreed against Mark—those of the so-called "Sayings Source." Those were my first tentative steps into New Testament scholarship.

Still, as I look back at those two semesters in Munich I have to admit that what most fascinated me was not the university: it was the encounter with art in its many forms. For me, Munich was a genuine "artistic intermission" between my previous studies in philosophy and the succeeding courses in theology.

My schedule for evenings often included concerts in the Hercules Hall of the Residenz or in the Congress Hall of the Deutsches Museum, or performances in the Prinzregententheater, the Residenztheater, or the Münchner Kammerspiele—mostly with discounted tickets. (For those coveted objects you had to stand in line and also be lucky.) Concerts, operas, and plays were a world that previously had been closed to me for the most part. Now I reveled in it.

Still, painting and graphics, both of which had thrilled me even when I was still at school, played an even greater role. An inexhaustible offering of works in those fields awaited me in Munich: the Alte Pinakothek, the gallery in the Lenbachhaus, the Schack gallery, the Villa Stuck, the Haus der Kunst with its rotating exhibitions and, not to be forgotten, the public graphics collection. The Munich Collection of Graphics is one of the most important in the world—and it was just there that, one day, I had a special experience.

That day I skipped the lecture of a well-known and deserving dogmatic theologian (who, however, usually read his lectures from his own books) and betook myself for the first time to the building where the Graphics Collection was then housed. I was the only visitor. One of the exhibitors offered me a comfortable chair, set up an easel, and asked me what I wanted to see. I was somewhat confused because I had been under the impression that I could pass by sheets of graphics behind glass and spend more time looking at the most famous pieces. So I said, somewhat haphazardly, "Dürer." "And what from Dürer?" asked the employee. "Drawings or prints?" "Copper engravings," I said, so as not to appear completely ignorant. "From what period?" the man asked. Now I had reached the limits of my knowledge, and I said: "Just bring me something beautiful." The man disappeared for a while and then returned with a heavy folder. From it he selected a splendid copper engraving, removed it from its protective cover, and placed it carefully on the easel; obviously I myself was not allowed to touch anything. He waited at a decent distance until I gave him a sign, and then he presented me with the next sheet from the folder. So it went on, all through the forenoon. After Dürer I looked at some pieces by Paul Klee and Max Beckmann—and felt like the king of Bavaria. That was the kind of thing one could experience in Munich then. I visited the graphics collection often, but still I never managed to see the whole treasure of 400,000 sheets by important artists to be found there.

Another, different "art experience" is still vivid. In the spring of 1957 there was a big exhibition of important paintings by the French artist Fernand Léger in the Haus der Kunst in Munich, and I visited it several times. Once I had the good fortune to be able to join a long guided tour led by an art historian. I was so captivated by Léger's pictures that I insisted to my fellow students, after I returned to the residence, "You *must* visit this exhibit!" Some of them did so; on a suitable day they accompanied me to the Haus der Kunst, followed me through the first part of the exhibit, and listened patiently as I explained the paintings. Then something happened that I had not anticipated: more and more people joined our little group, and suddenly I found, to my growing surprise, that I was speaking to a large number of visitors to the exhibition. Luckily I still remembered a lot of what I had heard during the guided tour. I must also have been speaking with quite a bit of enthusiasm. The group grew larger and larger, and followed me to the last picture. Back at home, of course, I was not spared some friendly teasing by my companions: "Well done, Mr. Artistic Guide!"—that was the most benign.

One day I visited the exhibits of the gallery owner Günther Franke (1900–1976) in the Villa Stuck and spent quite some time looking at printed graphics by Alfred Kubin. Suddenly Günther Franke emerged from his little office, introduced himself, asked me what interested me so much in those pictures, and finally inquired what my occupation was. "Theology student," I answered. "And what do you intend to become?" was the next question. I stuttered a little, because I did not like to be asked that and I did not expect much understanding, but finally I said: "A priest." Günther Franke broke into a smile, shook my hand, and said: "Let me congratulate you. That is a wonderful calling." He then invited me to his home on the following Sunday, where he showed me his collection of well-known Expressionists. Afterward, as he introduced me to his wife, she said to me, her eyes shining: "Just a few days ago we both became Catholics." There was an open missal on their table. I will never forget that encounter in Munich.

On another occasion I was moving through the little studio in the basement rooms of the Academy of the Visual Arts, and there I encountered a young sculptor who was only one year older than I. He was a master's student of Professor Heinrich Kirchner, from whom he had learned bronze casting (by the lost-wax process). We fell into conversation, and I later visited him often in his tiny studio; soon I was also a guest in the little rented apartment where he lived with his wife, Inge. She, too, was a student at the art academy and painted wonderful aquarelles of flowers as well as tiny, precious reverse paintings on glass. She was also a fabulous cook, and so there were any number of Sunday suppers at which conversation about ancient and modern art never came to an end.

Max Walter—that was my new friend's name—returned after the completion of his studies in Munich to his home village of Vasbühl in Main-Franconia and there, on the inner edge of an ancient quarry, he built a house with a big studio and bronze-casting apparatus. Many works of newer church art in Franconia and its environs are his: for example, the "Crossbearer" next to the cathedral in Würzburg. Later I often spent my holidays with him in Vasbühl, and in his studio I modeled small objects in wax that he then molded into bronze in his foundry. One memorial piece still stands on my desk: a cat, about 5.9 inches long, intent on catching a mouse.

However, as before, the question again arises: why am I telling about these things? What does it all have to do with my faith? A great deal, I think, because in that time I learned to *see* in a more profound way.

Certainly that had begun much earlier in my life. When I was still in school my parents gave me a double-lens reflex camera, a Rolleicord. The format was 6x6, so it was impossible just to snap around randomly. In the 6x6 format there were only twelve pictures on the then-usual film rolls, so one had to look carefully and consider what and how to photograph. Add to this that I was able to construct a little darkroom in which I developed my own films and enlarged the negatives. That compounded the intensive observation. I learned how to work with image details, to use photographic paper with harder or softer gradations, and in the very act of taking a photo to see the later image in my mind. My ultimate purpose was not to make *beautiful* pictures. I wanted to capture what was characteristic of a landscape, an object, or a person. To recognize that characteristic aspect it was necessary to look sharply and repeatedly.

All that was only a prelude to what happened during that year in Munich: I could stand for a long time in front of a painting in the museum in order to see how form and color functioned in it. Some paintings—such as those by Paul Cézanne or Max Beckmann—really captured me; I had to tear myself away from them every time. It was much the same when I looked at ancient sculptures: I went again and again to the grave stele of Mnesarete (380 BCE), moved by the beauty and, at the same time, the quiet melancholy in the face and figure of the dead woman.

Why are the so-called "visual arts" so fascinating? Why are so many people drawn to them? There are, of course, countless theories about this, but above all the graphic arts have taken on an unbelievable variety of forms since the 1960s. As a result, the concept of "art" has positively exploded in every direction. I think only, for example, of Minimal Art, Pop Art, Conceptualism, Performance Art.

None of that existed during my time in Munich—or it had not yet entered the art scene there. I developed a theory about the pictures and graphics I then encountered: graphic art—that is, art made to be looked at—either intends to *reflect* or to *newly create* reality. *Reflecting the world* was the classic form of graphic art. With the advent of abstract art, something new was added: now many artists wanted, on their own, to *create a new world*: in new colors and combinations of colors, but above all in completely new and radically abstract forms. However, as physics and chemistry probed ever deeper into the microscopic world and astrophysics into the universe, it soon became evident that the colors and shapes of abstract painting had already long existed in the real world—and were now become visible by means of the refined photography of scholars.

All the graphic arts that I then encountered thus represented "world"—either for reasons of magic or simply of curiosity, sorrowing or joyful, startled or admiring, provocative or comforting, intending either to change the world or to make it possible to rest within it—but always searching, extending itself, on its way to the still greater thing. That is why great art also awakens our longings. We cannot escape from it because it reveals our own hunger for what is eternal. Modifying a famous line from Nietzsche, we could also say:

> "All art wants eternity,
> —wants deep, deep, deep eternity!"[2]

I am not saying, of course, that the works of art in question should never be destroyed. Rather, in every successful work of art (and the same is true for music) the beholder (or listener) discovers her or his own hunger for the limitless. For every work of art—that is genuine art and not *kitsch* or soulless shoddiness—secretly reveals something that transcends the work itself: something nameless, ungraspable. It is in that sense that I learned to *see* during that time in Munich, and that is why the year has a great deal to do with my faith. I would not want to be without it.

[2] Modified from Friedrich Nietzsche, "Zarathustra's Rundgesang," in *Also sprach Zarathustra*.

7

Theology

In the summer semester of 1958, then, I was back in Frankfurt, at Sankt Georgen, and now my studies in theology were more focused than they had been in Munich: dogmatics, in particular, took up a lot of space. When I think back on that time it is clear to me that even then one of the most important questions in the study of theology was: how can one explain the frequently difficult and all-too-often-misunderstood concepts of the Christian faith in such a way that they can be accessible to the minds of people today? Now, my readers already know from the Preface that this book is not meant to be an autobiography in the usual sense. Instead it is meant to show, *within the mold of a personal biography*, that the faith given us by God and a truly enlightened reason never contradict each other. That, at any rate, is one of the main ambitions of this book. Therefore in this chapter I will not tell of any events during my remaining studies in Sankt Georgen. Instead, I want to speak about two central points of content in Christian faith: the *triune God* and *original sin*.

Neither of those matters of faith has let go of me since Sankt Georgen, and that remains so today. We can perceive two truths in terms of those themes: (1) Even the most profound mystery of Christian faith, namely, the belief in the triune God, requires "exertion of the concept."[1] (2) Our catechisms continue to speak about

[1] This idea ("Anstrengung des Begriffs") comes from G. W. F. Hegel; "exertion of the concept" is a frequent translation. Here we might instead think of an "expansion of the concept."—Tr.

"original sin," and that language is so misleading that no one can understand any longer what it is really supposed to mean. Those two themes will therefore be the subject of what follows—representative of many other things that were part of our program of studies. And the readers who will now enter on a somewhat lengthy road of "theology" will be accompanying me in my own explorations of the faith.

Christians believe in the *triune* God. That is what I learned in catechism class when I was eight years old. Let me begin right away with the principal difficulty: if we talk about God the Father, God the Son, and God the Holy Spirit, isn't there a great danger that these three will appear to be three gods? How can we make it plausible to a believing Jew or a devout Muslim that it is not so? And when we speak of the "one God *in three persons*"? Hence the question: what, after all, does "person" mean here?

In our normal understanding we regard every adult as a separate and discrete reality, responsible for itself. This clearly separable existence then, beyond itself, makes contact with other existent beings of the same kind, that is, other persons. If we picture the three *divine* persons in this way, obviously we have three gods.

However, even for the *human being* as a person the idea of a sharply distinct and distinguishable reality is only partially correct, because with regard to humans the question also arises: is this one, insofar as she or he is a person, really such an independent reality existing in and for itself?

To put it quite simply: how do we become *mature* persons? (In Christian understanding, of course, we are persons from the time of conception—but how do we become *mature* persons?) How—to put it in purely biological terms—does the original cluster of cells become the personality we encounter as an adult many years later? A development has occurred—indeed, an extraordinarily long and highly complex development. The things that have to happen are almost infinite; we cannot count all the elements that make up this process of becoming a person.

A child has to be nourished and cared for. Its parents have to smile at it and embrace it. Above all, they must speak with it. The care and attention of the parents are the first things that evoke the fundamental trust that is the basic condition for anyone to become genuinely human—and yet that is just the beginning. The child's range of vision steadily expands as it grows more and more into a dense field of relationships with a greater and greater number of other people. The language a child gradually learns conveys "world" to it, and it enters into an increasingly intensive relationship to that world, taking more and more of the world into itself.

What, then, is a person?—not only a reality resting within itself and oriented only to itself, but always also the sum of its relationships with other people and the world. All this is most powerfully visible in love, the turning of oneself to another "thou," entrusting oneself, giving oneself. Every human person, then, is autonomous and yet to an extraordinary degree is also "relationship"—and much more intensively than we normally imagine. We mainly suppose that we rest within ourselves, but that is not so. Essentially, we do not exist without the relationships that make us who we are.

Now let us make a kind of cross-check, eliminating from the story of our lives all the people we have ever met and with whom we have had anything to do: mother, father, spouse, siblings, friends, neighbors, all acquaintances, all our teachers, every person we have ever encountered. We will likewise eliminate all the books we have ever read, all the films we have ever seen, all the media that have ever informed us in any way, everything that has ever delighted us, and all the conflicts we have ever been involved in—in fact, everything in the world that has ever come our way.

What remains of us?—almost nothing but a skeleton. Really there is not even that, because we have eliminated the parents who begot us. Being a person, then, means in the most profound sense being-in-relationship. Without the web of relationships within which we have lived in the past and still live we would no longer be who we are; indeed, we simply would not be.

Now, theology says of the triune God that Father, Son, and Spirit are pure relations, pure "relationships." They are by no means realities resting within themselves but, to the extent that they are persons, nothing other than "relationship." The Father is pure self-communication and self-gift to the Son. The Son is pure emanation from the Father and pure listening to the Father. And the Spirit, too, is pure emanation and reception. Altogether, the one God is a "We" that is beyond our imagining. Thus the mystery of the triune God makes it clear that the last and ultimate thing is not "being-in-oneself" but "being-for-another" and "being-from-another."

But for this crucial difference in the concept of "person" in the triune God to be still more clear we have to take a closer look at the human being. I myself—my "I," my self—*do* things. I stand, I sit, I walk around the room, I eat, I go to bed at night. "I" do all that, but I am not simply identical with what I do. I am not just my standing. I am not merely the process of my eating. I am also not simply my going-to-bed. There always remains a center of activity that does or does not do things.

What theology says of the three divine "Persons" is that there is no such difference between them. God the Father is not first of all God the Father—and then does something in addition to that: God loves. No, Sacred Scripture says: "God *is* love" (1 John 4:8). That is: with God love is not something secondary, something added. God the Father is nothing other than the event of pure love. In just the same way the Son is nothing but pure listening, pure reception, pure handing-on of what is heard from the Father (John 15:15). Correspondingly, the Holy Spirit is nothing other than the bond of love between Father and Son, nothing but pure receptivity and communication of what is received (John 16:13-15).

I think these reflections show us that when we speak of three "Persons" in God the concept of "person" we use is profoundly different from the one we apply to ourselves. We can create some bridges to understanding, but we cannot form any other positive concept of the personhood of the Father and the Son and the Holy Spirit. The same is true, of course, of everything we say about God. We can only speak of God in images and comparisons, and in them the dissimilarity is immeasurably greater than the similarity. Even when we speak of "three" divine persons we must be clear about the fact that the number three is in this case a dissimilar concept—that is, something completely different from a statement I might make about three trees or three houses or three people.

The question, then, is: how did we ever come to believe in the one God *in three persons*? More precisely: how was it that this belief in the triune God could ever have its beginnings in Israel, the base of the most radical monotheism?

First there was Israel's experience of the one God who rescued this people from Egypt, journeyed with it through the wilderness, led it, saved it, forgave its guilt, is near to it. This is no absent, dismissive, faraway God. This is a close and saving God, a God who comes to the aid of God's people. Israel already called this God "Father." ("Father," too, is another of those "analogous" concepts: the dissimilarity to an earthly father is incomprehensibly greater than the similarity.)

This fundamental experience of closeness to its God, one that Israel always had, acquired a radically new dimension in Jesus, in whom God has finally and forever become present within the people of God. Jesus' disciples found no other way to express it. They had to say: Jesus is God's ultimate Word. In Jesus, God has said everything, and forever: in him God has fully expressed God's own self. In Jesus, God has also fully acted. In short: whoever sees Jesus sees the Father (John 14:9). And because Jesus is entirely the image, the reflection of the Father, they had to say he is the "Son" (Matt 11:25-27). But that does *not* mean Jesus is a "second" God; rather, it means that Jesus is the ultimate presence of the Father—the eternal "Word" of the Father—in the world. Therefore prayer by the people of God can no longer ignore him. All prayer to the God of Israel now takes place "with him" and "in his Name" (John 14:11-14).

On the day of Pentecost, then, all that is intensified by a third basic experience: Jesus is—from a superficial point of view—no longer present. His disciples can no longer see him. No one can still hear him. And yet—he is not separated from his disciples. He is in their midst (Matt 18:20). He is with them when they gather; he is, in fact, closer to them than he ever was before. He is with them through his Spirit. That is precisely the fundamental experience of Easter and Pentecost—and the church's basic experience *as such*. Through and in the Holy Spirit, Jesus is present, and with Jesus the Father's very self.

When the church no longer speaks simply of "God" without distinction, but of "Father," "Son," and "Spirit," that is not a subsequent construct, nor is it an ideology directed against Israel's belief in the one God. Historically, that would be completely implausible, because the experiences described took place *within* Israel, in the sphere of the strictest imaginable monotheism.[2]

Those who formulated the belief in the triune God were not Gentile Christians; they were Jewish Christians, firmly rooted in Israel's faith (think only of Paul). And the theologians who probed more deeply into the mystery of the triune God in subsequent centuries, in order to secure it against misunderstandings, did not think in the spirit of Greek philosophy. In that case they would have had to speak of a "primeval One" that is the absolute negation of all plurality—or, with Aristotle, of the "unmoved mover" whose thought can never be anything but *itself*.[3] To think of other than the self would be to lose its divinity. No, those theologians did not think in terms of Greek speculation, but in and out of the New Testament.

Faith in the Father, Son, and Spirit thus rests on historical experiences through which God revealed Godself. The *one* God has become present in the world in such a way that all previous divine becoming-present has led to God's goal and perfection. Therefore the Son and the Spirit are not two other gods; they are the dedication of the one God to the world in which God is now fully present—in the face of the Son and the power of the Spirit.

The accusation that we worship three gods is a slandering of Christian faith, and Christians' speaking of the *one* God in *three*

[2] Note that monotheism in the Jewish–Christian sense is not the *reduction* of a multitude of gods to a single one. God is in no way a part of the world, as are the gods of polytheism. God is not the sum of the world and its powers, not even the ultimate foundation of the world from which it flows. God exists beyond the world as the absolute Other who created it and therefore is not in any way identical with it.

[3] For Aristotle, God [whom he calls "Mind"] is eternally perfect spirit, existing from eternity from and through itself: pure thought. "But what does Mind actually think?" asks Aristotle, in the twelfth book of his *Metaphysics* (1074b), and he answers: "Mind thinks itself, if it is that which is best; and its thinking is a thinking of thinking" (http://data.perseus.org/citations/urn:cts:greekLit:tlg0086.tlg025.perseus-eng1:12.1074b). Given Aristotle's logic, what else could God/Mind think? After all, God is perfect being-in-itself. If God were to think anything else—according to Aristotle—such as human beings or some individual thing, God would no longer be thinking as the Most High; this would involve a movement away from Godself, and God's perfection would be lost.

persons is not contrary to logic; it is part and parcel of the insight into what a "person" really is. Every human person is made by *relationship*.

Are you still interested in following me through the rest of what I learned from my studies in theology? Then come with me to the second topic: the dogma of original sin. It is one of the church's most insightful dogmas, but it often creates wrong ideas. The idea that sin is "inherited" (German: *Erbsünde*) is a heavy burden. Regrettably, the idea of "inherited" sin seems firmly embedded in German-speaking populations—even in the German version of the post–Vatican II *Catechism of the Catholic Church*[4] (§§396-409). There the classic "original sin" is only mentioned in a parenthesis after "Erbsünde" (*KKK* §389). German readers, of course, ask themselves: how can sin be inherited?

Other languages are better off. In English the Latin *peccatum originale* is correctly translated "original sin." In French it is *péché originel*, in Spanish *pecado original*. Still, that does not take us much farther.

After all, the church teaches that through baptism a person—and obviously even a *baby*—is freed from "inherited sin" or "original sin," which is "erased" by baptism (cf. *CCC* 405). "How can that be?" our normal contemporaries ask. "Everybody knows that a baby cannot have sinned. An infant cannot yet act as a person. If sin is something personal, if it presumes knowledge, freedom, and responsibility, the little child cannot have become guilty of it yet." Why, then, this talk of "original sin" and "freeing from original sin through baptism"?

In light of these obstacles to understanding it is worth looking more closely at what the church in fact means by the concept of "inherited sin" or "original sin." I will first attempt to clarify it in terms of ongoing events that have troubled the world for some time now—namely, the pollution of the environment. Certainly

[4] *Katechismus der Katholischen Kirche* = *KKK*. English: *Catechism of the Catholic Church*. The enumeration of the paragraphs is the same.

"global warming" would be more current, but the concept of environmental pollution goes back farther and is therefore easier to grasp. There are some striking overlaps between "original sin" and the contamination of our environment, and those can show us what this dogma is really about. I will construct a kind of scenario.

Once—let us say in the nineteenth century—there existed somewhere in Westphalia a region where people raised grain. There were orchards with big apple and pear trees, and there were cows and hogs in the barns. Individual farmsteads were scattered among the fields and meadows, and every one of them had its own well, with its own pump to access groundwater. No canals and wastewater treatment plants existed, at least not in this rural district.

Toward the end of the century, because of the proximity of mines and the good access to transportation, industry moved in. After that everything proceeded very swiftly. Soon there were chimneys on the horizon, emitting carbon dioxide and sulphur dioxide into the atmosphere all year long. Toxic substances and waste oil appeared in large quantities; for simplicity's sake they were simply allowed to soak into the soil. Some of it was channeled into the brooks, which became increasingly foul. There was, as yet, scarcely any notion of "waste management," and the concept of the "environment" in its present sense was as yet unborn.

Later, in the places where agriculture had not been pushed out, huge quantities of insecticides were applied; no one was yet aware of their perilous nature. Beginning in the 1940s, DDT and other pesticides were sprayed without any restraint. The ground throughout the region was increasingly contaminated. The soil contained deposits of lead, cadmium, mercury, arsenic, and many other harmful substances. The fish in the brooks were long since dead or contaminated with mercury. The lettuce and vegetables in the household gardens were saturated with toxic metallic compounds. The groundwater pumped into the farmsteads made people ill.

There is no need to describe all that in detail. We can simply consider a child born into that situation. It is not responsible for the pollution of the environment. It can do nothing about the fact that it gets milk containing dioxin to drink. It cannot help it that the spinach its mother cooks for it contains lead. And it does not yet know that its constant coughing is due to chemicals in the air. To begin with, it is absolutely guiltless.

Those responsible are the ones who have recklessly poisoned the whole district, and even those who did so were not really clear about the consequences of what they did. We can learn three things, above all, from this environmental scenario to answer our question about original sin:

1. Every child that comes into the world in that region is "born into" an evil situation. It is completely innocent, but it is surrounded by toxic substances, and it absorbs them—into its lungs, its stomach, its fatty tissues. The poisons do not remain on the skin. The child receives them, willy-nilly, into its innermost organs. It cannot escape the situation within which it lives. That is simply a given.

2. The person placed in the situation of evil just described then "strengthens" it in turn. How? Very simply: until the middle of the twentieth century there was little or no sensitivity to environmental issues. We evidently believed our planet could swallow everything. It was only with the publication, in 1962, of Rachel Carson's book, *Silent Spring*, that people began to take note—in the United States, in Europe, and elsewhere. Rachel Carson had observed that for some years there had been no singing birds in the area where she lived. Spring remained silent. She had researched the causes and had discovered the consequences of the massive use of DDT in agriculture. Suppose that the person we spoke of lived *before* her book, in the time when there was not yet any enlightenment about environmental damage. That person would, as a child and as an adult, most probably have done exactly the same as everyone else: contaminated the environment. That is, as it grew up, the child would have participated in advancing the same negative situation into which it had been born and within which it had grown. It would have intensified the situation by its own actions. Thus if we consider the whole in terms of sin we may certainly speak of a "web of guilt." First there were the "originators," that is, those who started it all. They were partly guilty, partly innocent,

depending on whether they knew what they were doing. Then came the "accomplices"—those who cooperated, as a matter of course, with what others before them had done. They, too, like the originators, may have been guilty in part and innocent in part, depending on the extent of their insight. In any case there arose a web of guilt in which the share of genuinely personal guilt due to individuals could scarcely be determined any longer. The whole resembled a fabric in which countless threads run every which way and everything holds together somehow, though the "how" is hard to discern. And because there are always accomplices and tag-alongs, a potential for evil tends to expand and become more and more aggressive. That is connected with the phenomenon of *imitation*: what one does, the others also do. What everyone does, for the most part individuals do as well. The evil is (in algebraic language) "raised to a higher power." Even those originally born innocent are entangled more and more within the whole.

3. Something else can also be illustrated by the scenario of the contaminated environment: the evil situation described here resulted not simply from toxic substances that were thoughtlessly diffused or blown into the air. If we really want to get to the bottom of the whole situation we have to speak of increasing industrialization—the too-small character of many farms at that time, forcing the emergence of large-scale agriculture; the enormous acceleration of the birthrate; the shredding of the rural social network; flight from the countryside; homeless masses living in bleak neighborhoods; oppressive poverty for some, but the opportunity for others to create vast fortunes. In the nineteenth century the Industrial Revolution profoundly altered social conditions in many countries. As positive as industrialization was in many respects, it was just as dangerous in others. It not only brought good things; it also created "structures" that resulted in sustained evil.

4. Finally, we can say that talking of a context of evil always presumes a "contrasting image." Otherwise we simply could not speak of "evil"[5] at all. Today we know, and our predecessors may

[5] German *Heil* versus *Unheil*, something like "well-being" and "unwell-being."—Tr.

have guessed, what a ruined world means and what its consequences are. But there must have been someone, at some point, who saw that for the first time, in full clarity. At some time there had to be an American who realized there were no longer birds singing around her house. Obviously she was not the only one, but she was the first to articulate it in such a way that many people became aware and suddenly joined her in saying: "In reality our brooks should be clean and the air pure and our vegetables free from pollutants. Really, there should be birds singing in the springtime and larks soaring over the fields." That is what I mean by a contrasting image. And it means that without a contrasting picture the context of evil cannot be diagnosed. This insight is of the highest importance for theology, because the doctrine of original sin had its contrasting image from the beginning: Paradise. The narrator(s) of Genesis 2–3 even deliberately placed that contrasting picture before the readers' eyes so that they could grasp the full extent of the context of evil within which they were and are living. The question is only: did this contrasting image of "Paradise" really exist at the dawning of human history? Or is it, perhaps, the goal of all history? Does this contrasting image already exist, everywhere, when humans live and work together in solidarity as the people of God? Or does it only have a diagnostic function, being simply an aid by which readers can grasp their own situation? I will return to this question.

In any case we have come somewhat nearer, with this scenario, to what is meant by "original sin": *we are born into a context of evil in which we are, to begin with, completely innocent—and yet it governs and determines our whole lives.*

Obviously further distinctions are necessary with regard to original sin, but by this time it should be clear what is meant by a "situation of evil," a "context of evil," and a "web of guilt."

It is easy to see, of course, that original sin is not about chemistry but about the potential for guilt that has accumulated throughout human history. What the two have in common, however, is that we are all begotten into a baneful situation. Today there is not only an immense destruction of natural environments—it is a long time since I have seen a lark ascending from a field, even though I have been living in a rural area for decades; in my youth I still saw them "rise up singing"—but there are evil-causing "historical" forces that are much more dangerous still. Let us, then, cast a brief glance at history and its potentials for guilt and entanglement, parallel to our environmental scenario.

When a child comes into the world it is not born into a historically neutral space, most certainly not a space free from guilt. The world, the society in which we find ourselves, is to a considerable degree shaped by powers that mold our lives through their words and central ideas, their tricks for dulling our minds and their hidden seductions.

For example, there is the broad current of Nazi ideology. Obviously it did not begin with Adolf Hitler; its roots extend far back into the eighteenth century. And as we know, it continues rampant. Portraits of Hitler hang in more rooms than we suspect, and not only in Germany.[6] And it is not just a matter of Hitler-images and swastikas. There is also the broad spectrum of religious fanaticism, which has existed in every century and continues with hideous excesses right before our eyes. We only need to think of September 11, 2001, with the destruction of the World Trade Center in New York and the 2,753 people who were murdered there. We saw the two burning towers and the people who leapt from heights of three hundred to four hundred meters in order not to be burned alive. We also saw the hatred of those in Islamic lands who danced, gratified, in the streets when they, like us, saw those images on television.

There is the anti-Semitism (specifically anti-Judaism) that lingers throughout history, for far more than two thousand years, and in which Christian theologians are not only horribly complicit, but whose full fury they first released. The mutually contradictory reactions in the West to Hamas's terrorist act on October 7, 2023, show the degree to which anti-Judaism is alive there, and not only in particular regions. Instead, various social media have become dangerous conduits for anti-Judaism.

[6] It is worth reading what Carmen Rohrbach has written about images of Hitler in Yemen. Cf. her *Im Reich der Königin von Saba. Auf Karawanenwegen in Jemen* (Munich: Frederking & Thaler, 2012), 119–20.

I could go on at length with listing powers of evil in the world. They of course include also all the Western ideologies of a "comfortable society," the model of "absolute human self-determination," and the penetratingly propagated "cult of the ego."

The world into which a child is born is anything but neutral. It is already governed by a multitude of "rulers and powers" (Rom 8:38-39; 1 Cor 15:23-28). That is precisely what the church is aiming at with its doctrine of original sin. When it says that everyone is "born in original sin" it is *not* saying that newborn babies have already sinned personally, and most certainly not that children are begotten in sin because the act of generation is itself sinful. Rather, the church intends to say that children are conceived and born into a world that is already ruled by self-deception and manipulation, greed and violence, and many other powers.

Moreover, one must not imagine these "rulers and powers" that influence human beings from the very beginning of their lives as if they were something purely external and independent, lurking somewhere outside the door—one's outer world, environment, and surroundings. All too often the powers to which we are exposed penetrate deep within us and take possession of our inmost selves.

Even before a child leaves its mother's body it is often half-smothered by the worries, plans, intentions, ideas, and guiding concepts of its parents. Quite often they dream, even *before* the child's birth, of what it will become: a champion athlete who will bring wealth to the family; a status symbol with a university career; a substitute partner because the spouses cannot get along; or a parade object in which one can display one's skill at bringing up a child.

Clearly, it is not always that way. There are many children who are really allowed to be children. The examples I have cited are only meant to make clear that a child's shaping, formation, subjection to outward influences, and exposures begin very early—often enough in the womb. A human being is begotten and born into a history long since shaped by sin, and the outgrowths of that accumulated guilt surround it, not only from without.

The dogma of original sin is, as I have said, one of the most realistic and insightful of the church's teachings, and the church itself was aware of why it said, in the words of the Council of Trent, that original sin is transmitted not (only) by "imitation" but by "propagation" (Latin: *non imitatione sed propagatione*). We are "born into" the webs of guilt resulting from the sins of others, into the ancient burdens of sin that often weigh us down even at the biological level. We not only live in society: society lives in us, in our very center. How was it possible that the majority of Germans allowed a criminal like Hitler to arise? How is it possible that in the United States many people praise someone of unbounded ego like Donald Trump?

Everything I have said thus far is meant to show that what the church means by original sin is not a phantom, not a construct, not a figment of the imagination. As easily misunderstood as the term "original sin" is, the thing to which it refers had its starting point in tangible, observable reality. But at this point I need to return once again to what I said about the contrasting image of "Paradise." Must we really believe that such a counter-image existed as a genuine historical reality at the beginning of human history?

Chapters 2 and 3 of the book of Genesis tell how humans first lived in a paradise, how Eve allowed herself to be tempted by the serpent so that she sinned against God, how Adam in turn let himself be led astray through Eve with the result that they were both driven out of Paradise, and how their sin then continues in their descendants: Cain murders his brother Abel. And that is just the beginning of a long history of violence that encompasses everything (cf. Gen 2:4b–11:9). Ultimately, the church dogma of original sin takes its beginning from that story.

But modern biblical scholarship has long been aware that the story of Paradise and the original act of sinning form a "patriarchal narrative." That is: what was true of a whole clan, tribe, or ethnic group could, in the culture of the time, be portrayed in the figure and the life story of an ancestor. *The patriarchal narratives describe, as an event at the beginning, something that is true always and in every place where descendants of that common ancestor exist.*[7]

[7] I am here drawing on the work of Norbert Lohfink, *Das Jüdische am Christentum. Die verlorene Dimension* (Freiburg: Herder, 1987), 187.

That makes it clear that what Genesis 3 and subsequent chapters portray as a single sin and an enmeshing in sin *at the beginning of human history* is an interpretation of the situation of the world and that of Israel *throughout history*, up to the real present time. Paradise is thus a contrasting image intended to show how the world actually could and should be. So we need not believe in a paradisiacal original reality at the dawn of human history. That is precisely *not* required by the genre of "patriarchal narrative" that places present realities *at the beginning*.

We not only may but *must* assume, in harmony with evolutionary biology, that humanity developed historically over immense stretches of time, slowly, from within the animal world. The first "early humans" (e.g., *Homo rudolfensis*) are estimated by researchers to have emerged some 2.5 to 1.5 million years ago. Their development into *Homo sapiens* then required countless further steps—by means of *gradual transitions*. In the course of this long development into human beings the possibility of an initial freedom must have emerged, gradually and at first to a very limited extent. I am speaking of the possibility for this being, as it emerged from the animal world, no longer to be guided simply by instinct but to learn how to choose from among different possibilities. That was intimately related to an emerging understanding, a growing recognition—that peculiar recognition belonging only to humans that extends beyond every individual object presented to the senses. This opened new possibilities to emerging human beings. They could now become transcendent to new things: for example, what is right, what is appropriate, what is good.

What the church calls "original sin" should thus be imagined as *refusal*—refusal to take steps made possible for people by their increasing hominization: a greater and greater freedom to know the true and the good.[8] Original sin can thus be seen, in its personal refusal, as *remaining stuck* in animal mechanisms—which for hu-

[8] This observation, which is essential for obtaining insight into the theology of original sin, comes from Robert Spaemann's essay, "Über einige Schwierigkeiten mit der Erbsündenlehre," in Christoph von Schönborn, Albert Görres, and Robert Spaemann, *Zur kirchlichen Erbsündenlehre. Stellungnahme zu einer brennenden Frage*, Sammlung Kriterien 87 (Einsiedeln: Johannes Verlag, 2nd ed. 1994), 37–66.

mans means being "more beastly than any beast," because they could be something different.

That refusal, of course, did not happen with *one particular* human couple. It occurred at many places where hominization was occurring, and it still happens today. It led to the web of sin and guilt described at such length above.

In spite of all that has been said above, this is not all that needs saying about original sin. I have spoken of Genesis 3 and the subsequent related chapters in the Bible as a "patriarchal narrative" that transfers the contexts of evil being experienced in the present to the beginnings of human history and explains them from that. But there are also *positive* patriarchal narratives in the Bible, such as those about the patriarch Abraham. Here again, the now-present time is pictured in a figure from the beginning.

This narrative, however, is not a story of evil and refusal; it is about the ever-renewed exodus of Israel from what has gone before, its daring to trust, its fidelity to its God. Still, that means that there exists in the world and in Israel not only a history of evil, guilt, and the web of guilt, but also a history of freedom, mutual solidarity, enlightenment, growing knowledge of God—a history of obedience and unbreakable fidelity in faith. The Old Testament describes the strand of this "salvation history" in multiple scenes.

"Freedom from original sin" then means placing oneself within this long history whose real symbol is Abraham and whose perfection is Jesus Christ, so as to have a share in it. That is precisely what happens in baptism. It is the entry into a "counter-history" in which one can become free from the contexts of guilt that surround us. It is not as if the church, the enduring *locus* of this counter-history, consists only of those who have become free—of guiltless people, of saints. But it is the place where freedom from all the consequences of guilt is given *in Christ* and can be renewed again and again. To that degree, and only to that degree, is even a tiny child freed from "original sin" when it is baptized.

So much for the subject of "original sin"! Now, again, the question: why have I written at such length about belief in the triune God and about what the church really means by the easily misunderstood idea of "inherited sin" or "original sin"—when I could have told about so many experiences and encounters during my continuing education in Sankt Georgen?

I hope I have chosen what is more important. I have tried to demonstrate the seriousness of those studies: not only the question of the triune God and that of original sin, but all the questions that were dealt with in my theology studies were fundamental ones—about the inexhaustible depth of Christian faith, but also about reason. And my readers may have sensed especially in this chapter that it is possible to speak rationally about God and the world. God remains the incomprehensible mystery of the world, but that does not mean that those who decide to believe in God with the church have to believe in pure nonsense or live in a "God delusion," as the English zoologist and evolutionary biologist Richard Dawkins accuses Christians of doing.[9]

How things went after the time in Sankt Georgen can be reported very succinctly. Our course—altogether, we were fourteen candidates for the priesthood—continued in the seminary at Limburg and constituted our final preparation for service as curates and later as pastors. But something happened to me before we were ordained as priests by Bishop Wilhelm Kempf on December 8, 1960, in the cathedral at Limburg that was important—in fact, unforgettable for me.

I had decided that before my priestly ordination I would not simply complete the usual one-week retreat but would make the "Spiritual Exercises," which last for four weeks. Four weeks of complete silence, Bible reading, self-examination, and prayer. The classic form of those exercises comes from Ignatius of Loyola (1491–1556), the founder of the Jesuit order. Ignatius wrote a short book he called *Spiritual Exercises* in which he recorded his own experiences with God, together with instructions for all who desire to have such experiences.

[9] Cf. Richard Dawkins, *The God Delusion* (Boston: Houghton Mifflin, 2008). Let me refer to my argument against Dawkins in Gerhard Lohfink, *Der neue Atheismus. Eine kritische Auseinandersetzung* (Stuttgart: KBW, 3rd ed. 2015).

Certainly Ignatius was thinking of solitary retreats. Those who decided to make them would seek God's will for their own lives with the aid of a spiritual companion. The Ignatian Exercises are still offered today in that form, but it is most common that a larger group makes them together. Then the retreat master gives the whole group guidance for their subsequent meditations on Scripture but may also, in occasional private conferences, enter into the individual retreatants' concerns.

That was the form of my own four-week retreat as well. It was a group exercise with a fairly large number of candidates for the priesthood from various German-speaking dioceses, and it took place in Switzerland, in a very popular retreat house in the canton of Zug.

Unfortunately it was the case that the retreat master for my course stretched the meditation-aids beyond their time limits, making each of them a kind of "lecture" in which every possible idea might emerge—above all his private opinions about conditions in society and in the church. Thus, for example, he spoke at great length about the fact that Lutheran church steeples did not have a cross on top, but a rooster. (Apparently he, as a Swiss, was unaware that in Southern Germany it was the *Roman Catholic* churches that usually had a rooster on the steeple.) And, being Swiss, he did not say "Hahn" (rooster), but "Gockel" (cock), making a grating sound with his tongue for the "ck" that was beyond imitation. That kind of thing was funny, of course, and everyone laughed.

But the more those digressions expanded, the more I suffered from them. I wanted to seek God's will for the shape of my life, not listen to such lectures. I later learned that others felt just as I did. But in spite of the situation I did make my meditations on Scripture, reflected on my future path, and knelt for long periods in the chapel at eventide.

Then something happened that I would never have expected. At the end of the four weeks, as I stood by my heavy suitcase at the nearest bus stop and waited for the coach that would take me to Zürich, there fell on me an unspeakable homesickness for the retreat house and what had happened there, day after day. I was close to grabbing my suitcase and rushing back to the house. That homesickness was combined with an inner sweetness beyond description. Something had happened to me in those four weeks that the over-long introductions to meditation had not blocked. It may well have been the sweetness that God gives beginners so that they dare to trust and depend on God. Weeks later, during the celebration of the sacrament in the Limburg cathedral, I experienced it again.

8

Finally at Work

After our priestly ordination our class remained together in the seminary in Limburg for a short time; then each was given his first assignment. For me it was to the parish of St. Ursula in Oberursel, a town of about eleven thousand at that time. It is on the southeastern slope of the Taunus range, bordering the city of Frankfurt am Main. The proximity of the city was perceptible at night from the reflection of its lights on the clouds. Nowadays the skyline of Frankfurt is visible from Oberursel night and day.

My superior was Pastor Josef Hartmann (1889–1972), who was respected and loved in the town. Everyone knew him. While I and my fellow curate drove through the town in our cars (simply to reach the schools, which were in the outer suburbs), Pastor Josef went everywhere on foot. He tipped his hat respectfully to everyone he met and was repeatedly drawn into conversations that often developed into pastoral counseling. I learned a great deal from him.

As far as my own duties were concerned, I had to give religious instruction every morning, in the two highest classes of the primary school, the two lowest classes of the high school, and two classes in the local college preparatory school (gymnasium). I also had to look after the crowd of altar boys and a number of Catholic societies, including especially the "Kolpingsfamilie."[1] These duties

[1] An international organization founded in Cologne, Germany in 1850 by Adolph Kolping, a diocesan priest, originally to help young journeymen with

occupied many weekday evenings. Work with the youth groups was assigned to my fellow curate.

Most important, of course, was Sunday. The early Mass, winter and summer, began at 6 a.m. and was attended by all the day-trippers headed for the Taunus. The next Mass was at 7:30 a.m., and for it the medium-sized church was clearly too small. Then, at 9:00, there was the children's Mass, and again there was not an empty seat. The series ended with the so-called High Mass at 11:00. That was attended mainly by the wealthy and well-to-do Catholics in Oberursel who slept late on Sunday morning and took a late lunch.

In 1959 the German bishops had begun the Lenten action "Misereor" to aid the countless poor of the world by helping them to help themselves. A separate episcopal office in Aachen supported and guided the work. We in Oberursel, like all the parishes in Germany, emphasized support for this annual action in our sermons on the appointed Lenten Sunday. An extraordinary amount of money was contributed. One could sense the profound religious emotion of those who sought to help as they were able. Still: broken down according to the individual Masses, the 7:30 a.m. service yielded most of the collection, while the amount donated at the High Mass at 11 a.m. was paltry in comparison. I have often reflected on why that was so. Were those with higher incomes simply in the habit of giving larger contributions directly to the recipients—or were they being thrifty so that they could become still richer?

My work was in fact not made up entirely of religious instruction, time spent with the altar servers, work with different groups, and Sunday Masses. There were other things, and they were important. Every Saturday we three priests sat in the confessionals, beginning at 3 p.m. and often continuing late into the evening. During Holy Week so many of the faithful came to make their Easter confessions that we heard them for nearly two whole days. And they were good confessions. Evidently there had been an

job training, education, and housing. More recently outreach has been to immigrants and to self-help programs in developing countries. See https://en.wikipedia.org, "Kolping Society."

excellent instruction for confession in Oberursel for many years, because there were always a great number that testified to profound faith and a solid determination to repent and be renewed. That gave me my first real insight into the grace and power of the sacrament. Being freed from guilt—and from all the soul's burdens that are often connected with it—what a joy that is!

I experienced much the same among the many older and sick persons to whom we brought communion every month. There was not just the joy that the curate came to visit them; for most of them it was more than that, though it was almost never put into words. Still, I felt it when sick people pressed my hands or when I saw how intently they followed the liturgical actions.

Then there were the dying to whom I was able to give the last rites! Of course, the situations could be very different. There were sick people who lay with pale, haggard faces, no longer able to speak. One could only see how they tried to move their lips to pray the Our Father. And there were others who stood faced with certain death and yet received me with joyful eyes and a hearty greeting. Once I visited a woman who died two days later from cancer. On the way I had made up my mind about how I would speak to her and what I could promise her. That was superfluous. It was not I who consoled the woman; she comforted me with her solid faith.

I would have loved to remain a curate in Oberursel for a long time. It was there that I lost a great deal of the anxiety and shyness I had never really been able to shed before. But something else was in store. After two years of this work I received a letter from my bishop, Wilhelm Kempf, permitting me to study for my doctorate in theology. I had made no effort in that direction. I wanted to be a pastor. The initiative came from two professors who had been impressed by my graduation thesis in New Testament exegesis.

Still, when I received the bishop's letter I did not refuse. It seemed to me that a doctorate in theology was certainly worthwhile. In addition, I had a relatively long time to think about it, since Bishop Kempf had requested that, before my possible graduate studies, I would spend a year as school pastor at a Frankfurt gymnasium, filling a position that had suddenly become vacant. I happily agreed; soon I was back home with my parents in

Frankfurt. And now the strange providence in the whole affair: the position was at the Heinrich-von-Gagern Gymnasium where, eight years previously, I had completed my high school studies. Many of my teachers from that time were still there, and suddenly they were my colleagues.

I was responsible for Catholic religious instruction in all classes, from years six through nine (freshmen, sophomores, juniors, and seniors). That was quite a task—especially because I had never taught the senior classes before. When I got home in the early afternoon and had eaten dinner I was too exhausted to so much as think about preparation for the next day. I couldn't even read the daily newspaper.

Even so, it was a good year. I especially enjoyed teaching the lower classes, and I soon saw that it was a good idea not only to take parent–teacher conferences seriously but also on occasion to issue special invitations to individual parents. Many of them were very pleased to be invited because, of course, it was a particular kind of parent who sent a child or children to a "humanistic gymnasium" (college-preparatory school) where at that time (!) the students first learned Latin and Greek, and only then were introduced to English.

I had long and fruitful conversations with quite a few parents in those conferences, not just about their children. I experienced something that was confirmed elsewhere in future situations: it was precisely the girls and boys in whose faces and attitudes I encountered that hard-to-describe mixture of grace, openness, and joy in living—such young people truly light up—whose parents were always people who evidently lived in a happy marriage and were *believers* in a modest and serious way.

At the end of the year I left my students and my former instructors behind, with some regret, and went to look for a place to live in Würzburg as I continued my studies.

9

Graduate Studies

Why Würzburg in particular? At that time two professors were recommended to me as directors for my doctoral program in New Testament exegesis: Otto Kuss in Munich and Rudolf Schnackenburg in Würzburg. I had chosen Schnackenburg, visited him, and we quickly came to a mutual decision. He was prepared to guide me in my proposed program of studies, and he also agreed immediately to the subject I suggested to him for my dissertation: "Jesus' Ascension in Luke."

In retrospect I thank God for having led me to choose Würzburg, a decision that definitively laid the tracks for my future life. Rudolf Schnackenburg proved to be a wise and even-handed "Doktorvater," and he was always ready to help. He had such confidence in me that he immediately offered me a newly vacant position as his assistant, a job that was assigned by the dean's office of the Faculty of Theology.

I have no need to speak about Schnackenburg's scholarly credentials. According to Pope Benedict, Schnackenburg was "probably the most important Catholic exegete writing in German during the second half of the twentieth century."[1] That was evident not only from his excellent scholarly work but especially from the great number of his students. These included doctoral

[1] Joseph Ratzinger/Pope Benedict XVI, *Jesus of Nazareth: From the Baptism in the Jordan to the Transfiguration*, trans. Adrian J. Walker (New York: Doubleday, 2007), xii.

candidates not only from Europe but from Africa, South America, the United States, Canada, and East Asia. We met every week for an extended seminar in which a single doctoral student had to describe a recently completed part of his work. In addition, at determined intervals each of us had to visit Schnackenburg at his house and report on the progress of our work. Obviously, that system demanded diligent, ongoing effort from each of us, and the public discussions in the seminar had advantages as well: they goaded individuals to discover new ideas but also protected them from wild scholarly eccentricities.

As regards housing I had enormous luck. I found a home as chaplain in a large rest-and-recovery home for religious sisters. The house was ideally located, at the edge of the city: it was not far from the university but at the same time it bordered directly on a forested area with long walking trails. The sisters were from the "Congregation of the Daughters of the Most Holy Redeemer."[2] Of course no one in Würzburg used that fancy name; they referred to them as the "Ebrach Sisters," because their motherhouse was in the center of the old city of Würzburg, on Ebrach Lane.

I was to celebrate Mass in the big chapel of the home every morning. On Sundays a lot of people from the neighborhood also attended our worship service. Since from the beginning of my work as a curate I had developed all my sermons in written form, two books gradually emerged. They were called *Gott ohne Masken* [God without Masks] and *Glaube braucht Erfahrung* [Faith Requires Experience] and were published by Echter. Those Sunday Masses with the Ebrach Sisters are another part of my many happy memories of my time in Würzburg.

The rest-and-recovery home was full of sisters all year round, women who worked tirelessly in the congregation's large hospitals and therefore were in urgent need of some occasional rest and relaxation. Of course that called for clever and diligent sisters in the house who cooked, washed, and cleaned the rooms. They also brought the chaplain his daily meals in a little room directly beside the kitchen. Of course there was a lot of conversation and laughter. (Incidentally, I have never met so many happy people as I have

[2] In 1969 the name was shortened to "Sisters of the Redeemer."

found among religious sisters.) At some point I joked: "When I have my doctorate at last, the puppets will dance right here." Many months passed, and I had long since forgotten my joke. But there came a day when my dissertation had been handed in, read and reviewed, graded, and I had passed the oral *Rigorosum* exams in several theological subjects. I came home after the *Rigorosum*, put down my things, went to midday dinner—and there were two tiny mechanical puppets, lovingly dressed in doctoral caps and fine suits, dancing around on the table.

Of course I had to work hard before, at last, the puppets danced. I would like now to say a little about that work, and I will have to enter into some scholarly questions. But fear not, dear readers! You will not have to pass an exam on them!

For me it had long been a burning question: what is the appropriate way to approach the many stories about Jesus we encounter in the four gospels? They had a troubled history from the beginning. As early as the second century the philosopher Celsus had asserted that what they narrated was mainly a collection of independent creations by Jesus' disciples—and where, for a change, they reported something genuine they unwittingly revealed Jesus to be a cheap magician.[3] A hundred years later the Platonist Porphyry ridiculed them in similar tones.

Then, centuries after that, in the course of the European Enlightenment more and more scholars adopted the biblical criticism of Celsus and Porphyry and built on it in their own ways. The greatest impact on this round dance was that supplied by David Friedrich Strauss (1808–1874) in his two-volume work, *The Life of Jesus, Critically Examined*.[4] It enjoyed many editions and translations and shaped the consciousnesses of countless educated persons in Europe, including, alas, many New Testament scholars.

[3] Celsus's polemic against Christianity was called "The True Word (Λόγος Ἀληθής)." It has not survived, but it can be partially reconstructed from the many quotations by Origen in his work *Contra Celsum*.

[4] *Das Leben Jesu, kritisch bearbeitet*, 2 vols. (Tübingen: Osiander, 1835–36).

David Friedrich Strauss intended that his work should free the *reliable* information in the gospels from all *mythical* additions.[5] In principle he regarded as "mythical" everything outside the bounds of normal, everyday experience and the laws of nature (as then understood!). Therefore "mythical" components included not only the infancy gospels about Jesus in Matthew and Luke, as well as nearly all the miracle stories in the four gospels, but also all the Easter narratives.[6] And where did those myths come from? They are—in his own words—"only the subsequent additions [in historicized form] of a more intelligent and artificially elaborated subjective poetry."[7] And naturally Strauss thought that would take care of all the "subsequent [mythical] additions" as far as modern people are concerned. He asserted confidently that they no longer accorded with the enlightened worldview of the nineteenth century.

Obviously Strauss's theses met with sharp opposition. His concept of "myth" was questioned, as well as the idea that biblical narratives could arise out of an *undesigned subjective community awareness*. As seductive and opinion-shaping as Strauss was for many educated people in Europe at the time, he simultaneously seduced many believing Christians and their teachers into insisting on the detailed accuracy of the New Testament stories about Jesus. That brought with it its own problems. Let me make it clear by using an especially drastic example.

Our family bookcase held a thick book—551 pages long—that we even managed to rescue from the bombing of our house in World War II. I read it when I was fourteen, and I still have it in my workroom. It was a bestseller by Franz Michel Willam, *Das Leben Jesu im Lande und Volke Israel*, published by Herder in 1933 with successive new editions until 1960 and translated into eleven languages. (By the seventh German edition in 1937 it had already reached 44,000 copies.)

[5] In what I say about Celsus and D. F. Strauss I am following Marius Reiser's book, *Kritische Geschichte der Jesusforschung. Von Kelsos und Origenes bis heute*, SBS 235 (Stuttgart: KBW, 2015), esp. 18–25 and 43–63.

[6] Reiser, *Kritische Geschichte*, 43–45.

[7] Reiser, *Kritische Geschichte*, 43–45. See *The Life of Jesus Critically Examined*, trans. Marian Evans [= George Eliot] (New York: Calvin Blanchard, 1856), 1:155. Words in brackets added by LMM to correspond to the original as quoted.

What was admirable about this book was that Willam took seriously Jesus' existence *as Jewish*. Jewish ways of life, Jewish laws and customs were pictured in detail for readers—and that was anything but a matter of course in those years. Still, the book had its weak points. Willam turned the gospel narratives into a history of Jesus. At the end of the book he used the two Lukan accounts of the ascension (Luke 24:50-53/Acts 1:9-12) to form an impressive finale for his work—but in doing so he missed the mark in embarrassing fashion. Readers were almost dizzy as they swept higher and higher in the air alongside Jesus, while far below them more and more of the Holy Land became visible. As Willam pictured it:

> *For the last time Jesus blessed the group of the faithful. Then they saw Him soar above the earth, rising by His own power.*
>
> *From [above] the Mount of Olives Jesus saw, round about, the places which His sojourn on earth, from birth to death, had sanctified. To the east, at an elevation, He saw the pale brown desert of Judea, and beyond it the furrow of the Jordan: to the west, beyond the walls of the city, Mount Calvary; to the south, the plains of Bethlehem.*
>
> *The picture grows in expanse, the higher He rises. He saw the countless ridges of Judea, resembling an ocean with waves frozen solid; cities and villages nestle on the slopes and in the valleys; then Lake Tiberias, its blue surface encircled by a wreath of towns and villages, enters into the picture; He saw Nazareth on the plain of Jezreel. The higher He ascended, the closer the places He had lived in and visited crowded together, and soon the whole formed but one scene: the country of Israel, the country of the Redeemer.*[8]

That was how the book ended. As well-meant as this passage was, it unintentionally verges on satire, for one only needs to continue Willam's chosen scenario a few steps farther to make clear how nonsensical such a presentation is:

> *In the end Jesus saw the land beneath him only as a blue-green veil. Faster and faster he rose, and the higher he went the more inhospitable it became. Far above, out of an ever-darkening heaven, shone*

[8] Franz Michel Willam, *Das Leben Jesu im Land und Volke Israel: mit 33 vom Verfasser aufgenommenen Bildern* (Freiburg: Herder, 1936). English: *The Life of Jesus Christ in the Land of Israel and Among its People*, ed. Newton Wayland Thompson (St. Louis: Herder, 1949), 482.

> *the sun, increasingly bright and dangerous, and at the same time the atmosphere grew colder and colder.*

What is wrong here? It is that Willam ignored the literary genre of the Lukan ascension stories. Luke tells of Jesus' ascension entirely *from the perspective of the disciples who remain behind*. He *refuses*, in fact, to give an account of Jesus' heavenly journey *from Jesus' own perspective*. There were many examples in antiquity of the "ascent to heaven" narrative form, but Luke does not use it. Instead, he chose the form of the "rapture."[9]

Willam's text shows us that the gospels' Easter narratives could be easily misunderstood—in the direction of free invention that attributes everything possible to Jesus (thus David Friedrich Strauss), but also in the sense of a history of Jesus in which every detail of the text is taken literally (thus F. M. Willam).

However, I have just used a kind of language that I must immediately correct: we certainly must take the texts of the Bible "literally." The question is only: what, precisely, are the "words" of a biblical text? What does it mean to tell us? What is its level of discourse, and what is its form? Is it like a set of "minutes" listing a series of external facts that could also have been photographed, if photography had existed? Or does the text speak on a completely different level, formulating truth (sometimes even historical reality) by means of images and symbolic language?

What I have just said is true, in fact, for all texts we encounter anywhere, and not just for biblical texts. *We have to take every text literally—otherwise we have not understood it or do not want to understand it*. For example: if someone catches us stupidly bragging or showing off and says "don't stuff your mouth so full!" and we take that challenge literally, it does not mean that at our next meal we take tinier bites but that we stop showboating—because precisely that, and nothing else, is what the other person meant by that expression.

[9] The classic form of rapture narratives in antiquity, including the Old Testament (2 Kgs 2:1-18), can be summarized as follows: A person is snatched away, before the eyes of another person or a gathered group of people, and is placed in the world of God, or the gods. Sometimes the raptured person is hidden by a cloud; sometimes witnesses appear to confirm the rapture. In principle there is no narrative from the point of view of the person raptured.

This insight is extremely important for appropriate interpretation of biblical narratives. How should we deal with these texts? What kind of language are they using? What do they mean to say to us? But above all: may we simply subject them to our expectations—especially when they come from a culture that uses forms of speech that are altogether strange to us? Must we not allow such texts to speak to us first, entirely without prejudgment and mistrust—thus not always just posing questions about how they came to be, but above all listening carefully to discern what they mean to say? Questions of that kind (philologists speak of a correct textual hermeneutics) had interested me intensely for a long time. Here Luke's texts about Jesus' ascension seemed to me to offer an ideal field for research. After all, they are part of the hotly-disputed sphere of Jesus' Easter appearances in the gospels.

In this chapter I have already spoken of two extremes: either the stories of the empty tomb and Jesus' appearances are free inventions (D. F. Strauss) or they have been misunderstood as a kind of history of Jesus in which every detail of the texts may correspond to historical reality (F. M. Willam). However, that was a very superficial sketch of the various positions. As regards Jesus' Easter appearances the opinions of today's exegetes are much more subtle.

There has long been a position that exercises a certain fascination because it makes things easier for people today. It could be described this way: after Jesus' death there were no visions or appearances at all. Nothing unusual, certainly nothing ecstatic happened at that time. The disciples descended into deep mourning—but in the midst of their sorrow the meaning of Jesus' death was "opened" or "revealed" to them in a wholly new way. In modern terms they had entered a "situation of disclosure." Suddenly it was clear to them that "Jesus did not remain in death; he has risen and is with God. God has justified him against the condemnation of his judges in the Council." They thus encountered the presence of Jesus within themselves, together with the grace of his forgiveness. They were newly converted to the one they had abandoned. Only at a second level were these "experiences of disclosure"—in which, obviously, reference to Scripture also played a role—poured into the received mold of "appearances." Originally the Easter experiences had nothing visionary or ecstatic about them.

I consider this position *theologically* possible. It would not destroy Christians' Easter faith. It in no way excludes an action of God (or of the Risen One) within the hearts of the disciples.

Still, from a *historical* point of view the position is untenable. It is an accommodation to the mentality of the Enlightenment, which seeks to argue away everything that is unusual and extraordinary. But it is impossible to eliminate the basic form of the vision from Paul's experience before Damascus, for which we have his personal testimony (1 Cor 9:1; 15:8). The gospels, too, clearly show that we are dealing with typically visionary phenomena. Peter's vision (Luke 24:34; 1 Cor 15:5) began a long series of further visions, first to the group of the Twelve (Acts 1:2-3; 1 Cor 15:5), then to no fewer than five hundred followers of Jesus at the same time (1 Cor 15:6). This could already be a reference to the original Jerusalem community. At some point the visionary phenomena even affected Jesus' own family: it is said of James, "the brother of the Lord" (Gal 1:19), that the Risen One appeared to him (1 Cor 15:7). Finally, the long series of these earliest Christian visions also included that of Stephen (Acts 7:55). Thus we cannot avoid the historicity of the Easter visions or appearances. Incidentally this also falsifies, at least in part, the "myth" theory of David Friedrich Strauss.

The only remaining question, then, is: were all these genuine visions just products of the unconscious mind, or was the Risen One really showing himself in them?

It is often asserted today that the disciples simply could not deal with the fact that Jesus, their teacher and master, was no longer with them, and so in the depths of their unconscious there arose an image of a Jesus who returned to them in order to bestow on them pardon and peace. Added to this was the profound hope in the imminent reign of God that Jesus had planted in them. Could all that simply be over? No! The disciples' desires and fears, hopes and longings, were suddenly transformed into the certainty that Jesus had arisen. That certainty had eruptively forged ahead in the soul's innermost projections, in which the disciples then actually saw what they longed for and dreamed of. This purely psychogenic process extending into the innermost layers of the person began with Peter. He then, by means of suggestion, drew his friends along with him, and the result was a kind of enthusiastic chain reaction.

Christian faith has repeatedly stood fast against this emptying of the Easter appearances, thus making them to be *unusual* but purely *natural* phenomena. Defending against the position just described, it has stressed the supernatural character of the Easter appearances, emphasized God's real action at Easter, and underlined the genuinely revealed character of the Risen One, seen by his disciples.

Thus in the question of "appearances" there are likewise two sharply contrasting positions. On the one side there is the assertion that the Easter visions were natural phenomena produced by the imaginations or, more subtly, the unconscious minds of the disciples. On the other side is the traditional position, one of constant defense: no, the Easter appearances were nothing less than supernatural events in which God, or the Risen One, intervened in history through revelation.

Even at the time when I was writing my doctoral thesis in Würzburg I found this strict alternative questionable, and today I consider it completely misguided: here the *natural*, there the *supernatural*—that is an extremely unfortunate and in fact falsely constructed alternative that should long since have been overcome theologically.

When God acts on human beings they are not made the passive objects of divine action; God acts with and through them. That is: God does not eliminate the structures, laws, designs, and potentials of the world. Rather, God acts with their aid and in cooperation with them. Therefore a *genuine* vision is both entirely produced by the human being and altogether an act of God.

To begin with, a genuine vision is entirely produced by a human being: it is the bringing-into-play of that person's history, past experiences, knowledge, hopes, imaginings—and all that, obviously, in an unconscious process that the person in question cannot control and in which contemporary styles and determinate forms of imaging play an important role.

The time is long since ripe for us to again regard visions as genuine possibilities for humanity. Then, in fact, one can also take seriously the real possibility that God can speak to humans within human structures. For as every vision is entirely a human work, so it can at the same time be altogether the work of God, who then uses productive, imaginative human abilities in order that God may be revealed in the midst of history.

The ancient principle of the doctrine of grace, that God's action does not suppress that of human beings but, on the contrary, reveals it, must be applied fully to the inner structure of the Easter appearances. This means that the disciples' Easter experiences can be regarded *theologically* as really and truly appearances of the Risen One in which God has revealed the Son (Gal 1:15-16), and yet *psychologically* as visions in which the imaginative ability of the disciples shapes the appearance of the Risen One. The two are by no means mutually exclusive.

It is only by regarding the Easter appearances as just described that we can take them seriously in terms both of theology *and* of anthropology. Then we need no longer recoil at the assertion that visionary phenomena spread, as if in a chain reaction, after Good Friday, and that they are completely inculturated within the available imagery and language of the recipients at that time. Then, for example, we can understand the extent to which the disciples "see" and "hear" the Risen One and can even "touch" him.

Then no one need any longer shrink from saying that the evangelists work freely in their depiction of the Easter appearances, in a way that seems odd to us: for example, with motifs drawn from the Old Testament. To take one familiar instance, Acts 1:9 reads:

> When he had said this, as they were watching, he was lifted up, and a cloud took him out of their sight.

Such a cloud appears frequently in ancient narratives of being caught up to heaven ("rapture"). Probably that is where the author of Acts also found the inspiration for using this narrative motif in describing Jesus' ascension. But it is certain that the Old Testament also played a crucial role. Therefore this cloud is neither a raincloud nor a fair-weather cumulus cloud, neither a fog bank nor a kind of meteorological updraft. The "cloud" is part of biblical symbolic language that everyone familiar with the Bible understood at that time. After all, the Old Testament tells how a cloud accompanied God's people Israel, sheltering and leading them as they traveled through the wilderness (Exod 14:19-20; 40:34-38). The New Testament accounts of the Transfiguration also speak of a shining cloud (Mark 9:7 // Matt 17:5 // Luke 9:34-35). It is an *image* of the presence of God. God is close to God's people, is in their midst, travels with them and yet is the Hidden One who is subject to no one.

When Luke says of the departing Jesus that a cloud took him, evidently this pictorial language is meant to say that Jesus now enters fully and definitively into the glory of God. From now on, Jesus is hidden—and yet he remains close to his disciples: indeed, in their midst.

That kind of pictorial language has become unfamiliar to us, but the ancient church still commanded this uniquely correct way of reading biblical texts and used it as a matter of course. A man like Bishop Maximus of Turin (fourth/fifth century CE) never even dreamed of seeing the cloud in Acts 1:9 as a meteorological phenomenon. In a sermon on Christ's ascension he said, with magnificent incisiveness,

> The cloud that received Christ is the same as that from which the Father's voice sounded on the Mount of Transfiguration. Thus it was not a cloud that received Christ, but God the Father received his Son.[10]

"Forty days" is another example of the use of biblical motifs. Why does Luke say that Jesus appeared to his disciples only for a determinate length of time, just forty days? The answer I will now give, and that also played a role in my dissertation, will draw us deeply into the crisis of the post-apostolic period.[11]

"[He appeared] to them during forty days," Luke writes in the foreword to the second of his two volumes. Immediately before that he had written:

> In the first book, Theophilus, I wrote about all that Jesus began to do and teach until the day when he was taken up to

[10] Maximus of Turin, *Sermo* XLIV 3 (CCL XXIII, 179).

[11] Certainly there is another reason for Luke's restriction of the Easter appearances to forty days: he locates the descent of the Holy Spirit on the fiftieth day after Easter, the Jewish Feast of Weeks (Shavuot). Since, according to the early church's theology, it is the exalted Jesus who sends the Spirit, the Risen One's appearances had to conclude before Pentecost.

> heaven, after giving instructions through the Holy Spirit to the apostles whom he had chosen. (Acts 1:1-2)

In this foreword in Acts 1:1-3, written in the classic Greek style for forewords, every clause is firmly placed and every word is deliberate. Luke means to say that in the first book of his two, that is, in the Gospel, he had collected and presented the *whole* Jesus tradition. He had left nothing out. Readers cannot escape the impression that Jesus' activity extended not just until his Passion but to the very day when he was received into heaven. The author's intention is to show that Jesus' acting and teaching continued without interruption through his death and resurrection until his ascension. In the next sentence this final part of his working is then defined more precisely:

> After his suffering he presented himself alive to them by many convincing proofs, appearing to them during forty days and speaking about the reign of God. (Acts 1:3)

With these statements Luke gives the period of the Easter appearances an especially prominent and specific character. What is this special character, which appears nowhere else in the New Testament, with the possible exception of John 20–21?

To begin with: the time during which the Risen One appears to the apostles is clearly limited. It is thus marked as a unique period that ends in a unique way. Luke thus gives this time a special quality: Jesus walks some distance with disciples—probably a married couple[12]—toward Emmaus, listens to their questions, instructs them, follows them into their house, acts as host and breaks bread, speaks the blessing, and gives them the bread. Only then does he vanish (Luke 24:13-31). His appearance to the apostles later in Jerusalem is similar. The Risen One shows them his hands and feet, eats a piece of broiled fish in their presence, instructs and advises them, and then leads them toward Bethany (Luke 24:36-50).

Why does Luke shape the narrative in this way? Why so "physical"? Why does he have the Risen One say "a ghost does

[12] We may conclude this because only the man's name is given.

not have flesh and bones as you see that I have" (Luke 24:39)? Why does he paint such a realistic portrait, as if Jesus was with the apostles just as he had been before his Passion? Why does he thus define this time so clearly? But above all: why does he say so emphatically that he has reported "everything" that Jesus did and taught, from the beginning until the day of his ascension? One possible answer seems perplexing at first, but there is much in favor of it:

Luke, with all this, is apparently defending against Gnostic heretics who, even in his time, threatened the church and had already caused a great deal of harm. Since the discovery of a set of documents in the little Egyptian locality of Nag Hammadi (NH) in 1945 we know more about the Gnostic heresy than previously. Now we are quite sure that as early as the second century there were writings in which Jesus appears as the Risen One and teaches his audience the secret revelations of *Gnosis*—for example, in the "Apocryphon of James" (*NHL* I, 2),[13] the "Letter of Peter to Philip" (*NHL* VIII, 2),[14] or the "Sophia of Jesus Christ" (*NHL* III, 4).[15] Christian Gnostics sought in this way to place their absolutely heretical and completely unbiblical view of the world on the lips of Jesus, in order to establish them in Christian communities. For that purpose they quite often used supposed dialogues between the Risen One and the apostles. It is possible that Luke had already heard of such falsifications of the church's Easter traditions and therefore constructed his account of the forty days as a dam against the flood.[16] The following observations, at any rate, speak in favor of that view:

[13] Introduction and translation by Francis E. Williams, *The Nag Hammadi Library in English*, James M. Robinson, general ed. (San Francisco: Harper & Row, 3rd rev. ed. 1988), 29–37.

[14] Introduction by Marvin W. Meyer; trans. Frederik Wisse, *The Nag Hammadi Library in English*, 431–37.

[15] Introduction and translation by Douglas M. Parrott, *The Nag Hammadi Library in English*, 220–43.

[16] Does the attempt to identify the forty days in Acts 1:3 as Luke's counter to *Gnosis* collapse in face of the chronology? Thus far we have no direct sources for a heretical Christian *Gnosis* as early as the first century, but heresies and their structural argumentation may exist for some time before they are attested in writing. — Something similar is true of Docetism. The first clear and direct witnesses also come from the second century, but most scholars believe the conflict

1. In Acts 20:17-38 Paul takes his leave of the Christians in Miletus and Ephesus. He himself is in Miletus; he sends messengers to call the elders of the Ephesus community to come to him. In principle this is his farewell to the whole province of Asia.[17] The words Paul speaks in taking his leave (Acts 20:23-24) anticipate his imprisonment and death. This is thus a significant and solemn speech within the framework of Acts. Its central passage reads:

> . . . I did not shrink from declaring to you the whole purpose of God. Keep watch over yourselves and over all the flock, of which the Holy Spirit has made you overseers, to shepherd the church of God, obtained with the blood of [God's own Son]. I know that after I have gone, savage wolves will come in among you, not sparing the flock. Some even from your own group will come distorting the truth in order to entice the disciples to follow them. (Acts 20:27-30)

That is a clear warning against false teachers—who come not only from outside but from within the community itself. At the time when the author of Acts was writing, it was already a reality. It is striking that the Paul of Acts says in his speech that he preached "the whole purpose of God" in the province of Asia and concealed nothing.[18] That corresponds precisely to the foreword of Acts, where the author stressed having reported *everything* that Jesus did and taught. Such formulas are obviously directed against heretical teachers who put *new words* into the mouth of the Risen One: namely, their own secret teachings. The author of Acts never says precisely who those false teachers are.

2. The Pastoral Epistles (1 and 2 Timothy and Titus) are even clearer about this. First Timothy in particular repeatedly contends with the eruption of *Gnosis* in the Christian communities (cf. 1 Tim 1:3-7; 4:1-7; 5:15; 6:2b-5). At the end, the author calls *Gnosis* by name:

---

is reflected in defenses against Docetism already in the New Testament (especially in the Johannine writings).

[17] The Roman province of Asia included a region in the western part of modern Turkey.

[18] Cp. Acts 20:27 with v. 20!

> Timothy, guard the deposit entrusted to you! Avoid the profane chatter and contradictions of what is falsely called "knowledge" [Greek γνῶσις]; by professing it some have missed the mark as regards the faith. (1 Tim 6:20).

It was not just "some." Christian *Gnosis* swiftly developed into one of the greatest dangers to the early church, especially in Asia Minor.

3. We can also see from the following that Luke tried to erect a dam against Gnostic false teachers by using the sharply defined period of forty days. As we have observed, this author places extreme emphasis on the physicality of the Easter appearances. The Risen One walks with two of his disciples to Emmaus, and later he even asks for broiled fish. I can only see that as an anti-Gnostic barb, because it precisely contradicts Gnostic theology of redemption. The true Gnostics hated material things and sought to be freed from them. Matter and bodies were, for them, a prison. The world and matter did not come from the true God but from an evil demiurge. World and history had nothing to do with God, who was absolutely distant from the world and whom every Gnostic believed could be found in one's innermost "self." The world and history had to be overcome. It went so far that certain Gnostic movements forbade marriage and the begetting of children (see 1 Tim 4:3). The wicked world must be "starved" and thus come to an end. (There were, of course, Gnostic strains that did the opposite: their followers lived like libertines in every respect because they were convinced that their Gnosticism had already freed them from matter—and if that was the case, they could do whatever they wanted.) In any event: when Luke quite correctly emphasizes the physicality of the Risen One, that did not fit at all with the Gnostics' program for redemption. Thus there are reasons to believe that, with his depiction of the forty days, Luke was arguing against the heretics of his time.

Still, there was another critical factor that haunted Christian communities well into the post-apostolic period: the delay of Christ's return. That, too, was given a central place in Luke's description of the forty days. When the apostles ask Jesus, before his ascension, whether he will now restore "the kingdom to Israel"

(Acts 1:6), Luke is already touching on that problem, and when the Risen One responds: "It is not for you to know the times or periods that the Father has set" (Acts 1:7), that is an initial answer. It becomes still more concrete when Jesus continues:

> But you will receive power when the Holy Spirit has come upon you, and you will be my witnesses in Jerusalem, in all Judea and Samaria, and to the ends of the earth. (Acts 1:8)

According to Sacred Scripture the outpouring of the Spirit is a clear and vivid sign of the end-time (Joel 3:1-5). When Jesus announced the imminent coming of the Holy Spirit, the disciples must have been gripped by eschatological expectation—and yet that apocalyptic anticipation of the end-time is immediately rejected. Instead, Luke sketches in masterful form what his second book will tell: for the present there is no longer any room for Jesus' return. It is now about witnessing to Jesus throughout the world, similarly to Matthew 28:16-20. The last and ultimate answer to the disciples' question about the nearness of the *parousia* is then given by the two interpreting angels:

> "Men of Galilee, why do you stand looking up toward heaven? This Jesus, who has been taken up from you into heaven, will come in the same way as you saw him go into heaven." (Acts 1:11)

Thus it is clear what Luke wants to tell the readers about the second crisis of the community in that time: it is completely mistaken and senseless to wait for Jesus' return, to cobble together possible deadlines and simply to wait with our hands in our laps. Real, lived witness to Jesus, his deeds, his words: that is the duty of disciples in this age of the world. Jesus will certainly return, but now the church is living in the time when he must be "witnessed" to. In a basic sense that also stands in opposition to the Gnostic heretics who constantly thought only of themselves and their own redemption—but *not* of the redemption and liberation of the world, which in any case is only trivial, unclean, and wicked.

So much for my doctoral dissertation. Obviously I had to do a great deal more than merely discussing the anti-Gnostic line of interpretation I have just sketched. For example, I spent weeks in the Institute for Classical Philology in the University of Würzburg collecting, interpreting, and grouping all the ancient and early Jewish literary texts on flights to heaven, raptures, and apotheoses.

Clearly I also had to gather, examine, and at least partially document the whole of the scholarly secondary literature on my topic. The final phase of that review of the secondary literature, however, no longer took place in Würzburg, but largely in Rome, since the Pontifical Biblical Institute there holds one of the world's best libraries for Old and New Testament. At that time I lived close to the institute for weeks, read literature on the ascension from morning to night, and in the process reviewed and corrected my already finished manuscript.

Not very far from the Biblical Institute lies the Piazza Navona, with one of the best ice cream shops in Rome. Not one evening passed but that the exhausted doctoral candidate, with a large cone in his hand, enjoyed the colorful life of this broad, baroque-influenced square. But eventually that time was over, the work was done, the *Rigorosum* exam passed, and the puppets were dancing.

It took me a number of years to get to that point. Still, during that relatively long period of time I was doing other things besides my doctoral dissertation. I wrote something else on the side, namely, a book called *Paulus vor Damaskus*.[19] The author of Acts tells of Jesus' appearance to Paul no fewer than three times (Acts 9:1-19; 22:3-21; 26:9-18), and differently each time. In this book I tried to show why the story was told *with variations*: in antiquity it would have been a serious artistic error for a good writer to tell the same story three times, all of them identical. The same was

[19] *Paulus vor Damaskus. Arbeitsweisen der neueren Bibelwissenschaft dargestellt an den Texten Apg 9,1-19; 22,3-21; 26,9-18*, SB 4 (Stuttgart: KBW, 1965). English: *The Conversion of St. Paul: Narrative and History in Acts*, ed. and trans. Bruce J. Malina, Herald Scriptural Library (Chicago: Franciscan Herald Press, 1976).

true, of course, of the two ascension stories, one at the end of Luke's Gospel and the other at the beginning of Acts.

Besides that, I gave lectures on the Bible in every possible place within the diocese of Würzburg. Those also required preparation. One of them I remember so vividly that I simply have to tell about it.

One of the pastors in Würzburg invited me to give an evening talk on the correct way to interpret biblical texts. We agreed that the topic would be "The Creation Account at the Beginning of the Bible (Gen 1:1–2:4)." I had also told him that I needed a large, stiff paper or a blackboard for a drawing. I arrived early at the parish hall in Versbach, a suburb of Würzburg. It was a big room with a high stage for theatrical productions. Unfortunately, all I had for my drawing was a heavy wooden board with an iron frame like those commonly found, in those days, on the front walls of school classrooms—but this one was not attached to a wall; it had to be set up in a makeshift way. On the stage, which was about three feet high, we placed a huge table, and on top of it two chairs; we leaned the board against the backs of the chairs.

On the board I had made a sketch in bright colors of the Near East as imagined at that time, including Israel (Gen 1:6-10, 14-18): the earth as a disk, with the "firmament" arching above it, a gigantic half-globe. Under the earth-disk were the "waters beneath" and above the firmament were the "waters above"—the heavenly ocean whose blueness we see from below. From there, rain falls on the earth.[20] In the firmament itself were sun, moon, and stars.

We were still setting up the board when the first members of the audience arrived. The big hall filled fast with, as soon appeared, an alert and deeply interested gathering. The pastor introduced me and I began my lecture. The lectern was not on the stage, but in front of it—directly below the elevated board. My lecture was meant to show that Israel's theologians who wrote the creation account in Genesis 1 based their story on the Babylonian idea of the world, but at the same time they radically changed it. For example, the stars in the account of creation in Genesis 1 are no

[20] See Gerhard von Rad, *Genesis: A Commentary*, OTL (Louisville: Westminster John Knox, 1973), 46–61, esp. 53–54.

longer gods, as they were throughout the ancient Near East; they are simply "lamps" that God fixes in the firmament. With this mode of presentation I wanted to show how, here, the Babylonian heaven of the gods was demythologized and even ridiculed. Babylon's holy, highly revered gods were degraded and just called light fixtures.

Since I had already given this talk a number of times in different places, I spoke quite freely. The audience followed well; I found myself constantly looking into attentive and excited faces. And then it happened: I was at the peak of my performance when I suddenly saw the eyes of the audience widen. I jumped to the side—I do not know what drove me—and the heavy, iron-bound board fell right where I had been standing. Our installation up on the stage had been a ludicrous improvisation. Dead silence filled the hall for an instant—and in that silence a man shouted: "That was the revenge of the Babylonian gods!" Then the audience began to cavort and shed the tension, amidst unending laughter.

So much for the years of my doctoral work! Obviously I have to answer the question with regard to those years as well: what did they mean for my belief in God? The answer can only derive from the fact that for years I occupied myself intensively with biblical narratives. How did I come to terms with this constant testing, critique, and often dissection of texts? Did that work damage my faith, or did it strengthen it?

Certainly it is true that in the course of my work the question constantly arose, directly or indirectly: what kind of texts *are* Luke's Easter narratives, including the two depictions of the ascension? Are they documented accounts? Most surely not. Or are they pure invention, novelistic narratives born of Luke's imagination? Certainly not that either. But then, what are they? What should I call this kind of text, this peculiar way of telling a story?

In my researches I never doubted that Luke 24 and Acts 1 contain fictional elements, but they surely did not arise out of Luke's independent imagination. The Easter visions of Jesus' disciples, with their command to missionize, certainly occurred—we only have to remember what Paul reports in 1 Corinthians 15. Likewise, the Gnostics' reinterpretation of the church's fund of tradition certainly happened—just like the long-enduring question about when the day of Christ's return will finally arrive. Thus there are real events behind both of the ascension texts, above all the unquestionable reality of the Easter appearances—but at the same time there are the questions, crises, and problems of Luke's church, which are meant to find an answer by means of the way he tells the whole story.

It became more and more clear to me that this was truly a unique form of text: not the kind we would hope to see on the front page of a serious newspaper, containing pure facts and detailed documentation of them. But it is not the kind we encounter in serialized stories in the features section. It is, in fact, a unique kind of narrative, working with fictive and possibly also nonfictive narrative elements. With their aid it consolidates real experiences of the disciples, and of the people of God.

When I began my studies in theology we were all excited by the question of the historicity of such narrative texts in the Bible. Foremost for us were the distinguishing of sources, genre criticism, historical criticism, and above all the search for the historical Jesus. That all made good sense; we did not dare fall prey to the snares of fundamentalism.

But above all during my years in Würzburg, in my efforts to understand Luke's ascension texts, I grew out of those questions. They were now less important to me. What interests me, and many other exegetes today, is the *final text*—not its prehistory but the text itself: its makeup, its structure, its progression, its theology, its sober character and yet, at the same time, the brilliance of its statements. It is about what the text wants to move me to do and what it means to say to me, so gently and yet so urgently.

What power there is in the simple statement: "You will be my witnesses in Jerusalem, in all Judea and Samaria, and to the ends of the earth" (Acts 1:8). It is only a brief sentence, but it is full of reality. Jesus' message has, in fact, reached the "ends" of the earth. Yet at the same time we are dismayed when we read that statement. How is it, in fact, with our witness to the Risen One?

I notice more and more often that today I read the texts of Sacred Scripture with a kind of "second naïveté." I experienced the "first naïveté" in my childhood; at that time the biblical texts were still full of magic. During my theology studies they were then dismantled, analyzed, separated, dissected, questioned, and systematized. Every theologian has to go through something like that—at any rate, I did it and thoroughly enjoyed it. That phase culminated with my theological studies at Sankt Georgen. But in the course of my further studies in Würzburg that kind of decompositional encounter with the biblical texts was already being blown apart. From that point on I learned in many, often very small steps how to let myself be led by the text without abandoning scholarship in the process.

Today, then, in my old age, I like once again to read my Bible quite simply. I carry the burden of scholarship with me, in my rucksack. It is necessary. It has to be brought along, because it helps us precisely with the task of really grasping the text in its final form. And still, today I can let myself be drawn in by the text itself and its power. I rejoice in it. I shrink from its claims. I let myself be consoled by it. I live with it like a child whose mother tells it stories at eventide.

I began to learn all that during my time in Würzburg, but that period continued somewhat longer. Even before I held my doctoral certificate, written in the most solemn ceremonial Latin, the question of a possible *Habilitation*[21] had arisen. Professor Schnackenburg gave his support, the faculty had no difficulty with it, and my bishop granted his permission.

So I began this new endeavor immediately. This time it had to proceed more rapidly, as is the nature of a *Habilitation*: the candidate must, above all, show that s/he is in a position to deliver scholarly lectures, so that her or his teaching ability (*facultas docendi*) may be officially established. In addition, a scholarly work must be presented and a test lecture given.

Since I had already worked my way through Luke's two volumes, I remained with them. Two years later I was able to present a book entitled *Die Sammlung Israels. Eine Untersuchung zur lukanischen Ekklesiologie*.[22] It was much thinner than the doctoral dissertation, but its subject was more important.

[21] A second "doctorate," this one oriented to teaching one's doctoral subject at the university level. A person with such a degree bears the title "DDr."—Tr.

[22] *The Gathering of Israel. A Study in Lukan Ecclesiology*.

In the course of my research on Jesus' ascension I had already encountered something that had been noted by many New Testament scholars: in certain parts of his two-volume work Luke deliberately writes in a style derived from the Greek Old Testament, the Septuagint. For example, he loves expressions such as "And it came to pass, that . . ." or "And behold . . ." Such phrases appear at many places in Luke's Gospel, but they are especially frequent in the beginning of the two volumes: that is, in the "prehistory" in Luke 1–2.

Why is that? What did Luke mean to achieve by using this stylized language? It would initially have sounded odd and even strange to Greek ears. But the answer is not difficult. For Luke this very different "Septuagint style" meant: this is a narration of *sacred history*—from the creation of the world to the prophecies in the book of Daniel. By seizing immediately on Old Testament style, at the beginning of the two-volume work and repeatedly afterward, Luke wishes to make clear that the very sacred history told in the Old Testament continues with John the Baptizer and with Jesus—and even beyond Jesus' death in the work of the apostles and Paul.

But that is by no means everything that needs to be said. In my *Habilitation* book I wanted to show that this *linguistic style* that appears again and again in the Lukan writings corresponds to a continuing *theme: the coming-to-be of the church as a long process of gathering and dividing*. According to Luke the process began already in the Old Testament; after all, the long speech by Stephen in Acts 7:1-53 is meant to show that Israel's resistance to Jesus, and now to Stephen, had a long prehistory. People in Israel had always been stiff-necked and resistant to the Holy Spirit (Acts 7:51). But it was equally true that there had always been people in Israel who lived righteously and faithfully before God (Luke 2:25). That is precisely what the prehistory at the beginning of Luke's Gospel (Luke 1:5–2:40) is meant to recall. By no means least, it functions to depict faithful Israel waiting for liberation and redemption.

Then, according to Luke, this process of gathering and separation continued in the Baptizer's movement (Acts 13:24)—then in that of Jesus (Luke 13:34), in which the mission of the Twelve to all Israel plays a crucial role (Luke 9:1-6)—and then with the reception of the Spirit by the disciples, which led first to their work of mission in Israel (Acts 2:14–9:43) and there, too, to gathering and separation.

Luke very skillfully links this development, in which part of Israel rejects Jesus' message but part of Israel is gathered, to the last part of the path to the church: namely, the reception of Gentiles. That for Luke the Gentile mission is still part of the Israel theme is evident from the quotation of the prophet Amos in James's speech in Acts 15: the fallen tent of David (that is, Israel) will now (in this time after Easter) be rebuilt, so that Gentiles also may seek God (Acts 15:13-18).

With all that Luke offers a picture of the church that is thoroughly considered. The church stands in unbroken continuity to Israel. In the process of gathering and separation, in which John the Baptizer, then Jesus, and then the Pentecost event play a crucial role, church *becomes*, it *gathers* itself. Luke has no thought of the church's being founded by a single action at some particular point. The whole process he narrates is the "work of God" (Acts 5:38-39; 13:41; 20:28). *And the church is the true eschatological Israel.*

When I submitted this work for my *Habilitation* I was, of course, aware how explosive it was. Many Christians, after all, have no conception of what it means to say that the church is and remains *Israel*. Otherwise they would not have such a broken relationship to the Old Testament; otherwise the Old Testament reading would not be so frequently omitted during Mass; otherwise even Vatican II would not have referred to the church as "the new Israel"[23] at crucial points. That unfortunate phrase created a rupture between the church and Israel.

As regards my own career, everything moved very swiftly after that; I can only regard the details as providential. A doctoral student from the United States who was writing his dissertation for Schnackenburg had a brother who was studying with Professor

[23] Cf. *Lumen Gentium* 9; 10; 13; 26, as well as *Nostra Aetate* 4; *Ad Gentes* 5 ("new Israel"). For a thorough historical and theological discussion of the syntagm "New People of God," let me refer to Tamás Czopf, *Neues Volk Gottes? Zur Geschichte und Problematik eines Begriffs*, MTS II, 78 (St. Ottilien: EOS, 2016).

Walter Kasper in Tübingen. Professor Kasper told his doctoral student, and the student told his brother, and the brother told me, that a junior professorship for "Introduction to the New Testament" in the faculty of Catholic theology was about to become available and the faculty were not satisfied with any of the candidates who had appeared thus far.

So I inquired of Professor Kasper whether it would make sense for me to apply. He referred me to the dean; I wrote to him, and he asked me simply to send him all my documents. I did so, and not long afterward I received an invitation to Tübingen for a "Vorsingen" (that is, a sample public lecture in the presence of the whole department: students and professors). I could suggest three topics, and I formulated my proposal in such a way that one of the three was certain to be selected. It was entitled: "Jesus' Prohibition of Divorce and its Addressees." I was not mistaken: that was precisely the topic that was chosen.

Two weeks later I traveled to Tübingen, for safety's sake not by car but on the train and, again for the sake of security, I appeared two hours early in front of the Kupferbau,[24] where the lecture was to be held. I looked around and saw a cemetery. "Ah," I thought, "there's a place where you can walk around and get yourself in the mood for the lecture." I did so—and suddenly I found myself standing in front of the grave of Friedrich Hölderlin. I stood there for a long time. Echoes of his poetry arose within me, faded away, and suddenly "Heidelberg" was in Tübingen:

> Shrubs cast down their blooms
> to the place in the joyous vale
> reclining on the hills or on the fair riverbank
> your merry lanes rest below fragrant gardens.[25]

This encounter with Hölderlin, one of my best-beloved German poets, was infinitely comforting. It was as if all my tensions and fears had been blown away. I said to myself: even if the talk turns

[24] Literally the "copper building," housing the principal lecture halls at the University of Tübingen.

[25] Translation by LMM.

out to be unsuccessful, I was at Hölderlin's grave, and that made the trip worthwhile. But it was by no means unsuccessful. A few weeks later I was able to accept the position in Tübingen.

Once again I needed to find a place to live. I did it with enthusiasm, because my parents wanted to come live with me and keep house for me (my father was then 73, my mother 72). So I had to find a spacious dwelling, something that was scarcely to be had in Tübingen itself. The only suitable and affordable places were in the surrounding villages—and here I encountered, for the first time, a characteristic feature of Swabian culture.

I put an ad in the paper, and through it I found a couple who worked for Daimler (no one there says "Mercedes Benz"), but who had a "side business" as well: a farm where they raised calves. They also had two children, and though the children were not yet of school age they had already made provision for their future, building a beautiful single-story house for them on the outskirts of the village of Öschelbronn/Gäufelden. "For later, when they are big!" they said proudly. We were able to rent the whole house, and at an acceptable price. A new season of life began for me.

10

Tübingen

There was a certain drama to the beginning of this new phase of my life, because I could not choose the topic of my first semester's lectures; it had been set by my predecessor and was already in the catalogue. The title was "Text, Canon, and Hermeneutics," and I had to prepare new material for the series in every detail.

My first task was to describe how the text of our contemporary translations of the Bible came to be—since, obviously, we no longer have the original texts of the individual biblical books but only copies of the originals. It is even more complicated than that: what we have are copies of copies of copies and, quite naturally, errors crept into the writing along the way. There are also deliberate "improvements" from copyists who thought they knew better or could produce an improved phrasing. There are textual variants for practically every sentence in the Bible (especially in the New Testament), and biblical scholars have to reconstruct the text in light of the oldest and best manuscripts, evaluating all the variants of the original. The first part of this semester was supposed to show how that is done.

Now, as I am writing this book fifty years later in a village near Munich while my thoughts have drawn me back to Tübingen, it is understandable that I got the idea of re-reading the beginning of the lecture series on "Text, Canon, and Hermeneutics." I hauled a huge box containing the manuscripts of my Tübingen lectures out of the basement of my present lodgings and brought it upstairs. Filled with nostalgia and curiosity, I celebrated the reunion and looked through the thick manuscript of my first lecture course in Tübingen. The whole thing was organized in forty sections. I looked especially closely at the first paragraphs—that is, the first single lecture—and I made an odd discovery. Most of this lecture was written in calm, easily readable lines, but in the latter part my writing became hasty, full of abbreviations, and scarcely legible anymore. Suddenly, the memories arose.

The time before my first scheduled lecture had been fairly hectic. I had to find a house for us to live in; I had to organize the move of my elderly parents from Hesse to Swabia as well as my own move from Franconia. That involved dealing with every possible incidental connected with moving. Then, to top it off, on the morning of my first lecture I was suddenly summoned to the office of the university's president. He wanted to give me his official greetings and hand me my certificate of appointment in person. But at that point the first lecture was by no means finished.

Looking back, I see myself sitting in the president's outer office, my hand flying as I scribble keywords for the second part of my imminent lecture. The secretary offers me a cup of coffee and watches my agitated writing with curiosity. I forget my surroundings and I write, and write—until the president emerges from his office and says goodbye to another visitor. After our meeting I go directly from the president's office to the lecture hall in the Kupferbau, where over a hundred students await me. Would they even listen?

They did listen. I began by reading them a text from a book edited by Karlheinz Deschner entitled *Was halten Sie vom Christentum?* [What Do You Think of Christianity?] in which eighteen authors were asked to say what they thought of Christianity. The essay by the famous writer Arno Schmidt, who had been heaped with honors in Germany, was entitled "Atheist? Certainly!" and contained these words, along with many other stupidities:

> It is high time, once again, to tell Christianity what an impartial witness thinks of it. . . . My answer to the question "what do you think of Christianity?" is . . . "Not very much!"—The sufficient reasons (as far as I am concerned) are threefold. First, there is the questionable nature of the foundational text

> (that is, the Bible; anyone who flinches here need read no farther). Then comes the (for me) inadequate person of Jesus of Nazareth. Finally, there is the observation of the effects of Christianity within its sphere of influence . . . during the past two millennia. *Avanti!*
>
> As long as anyone proclaims as the purest source of "divine truth," the holy norm of the "most perfect morality," and the basis for state religions a book that has—at an indulgent reckoning—50,000 textual variants (thus presenting, on average, thirty controversial passages per printed page . . .): so long as that continues, we deserve the governments and conditions we have.[1]

"There is no way," I said to my listeners after reading that text to them, "to speak more stupidly about the textual history of the Bible, for the great number of textual variants[2] results from the fact that this book derives from countless manuscripts, many of them very old—incomparably more than the works of all other authors from antiquity. Given the great number of manuscripts, there are obviously many more text variants. Besides, most of them involve unimportant details that do not change the meaning of a verse in the slightest. Moreover, in the vast majority of cases they can be explained and set aside after a consideration of their text families and by means of textual criticism of their content. Especially in the New Testament we have an extremely reliable text that, in addition, is affirmed by quotations in early church authors.—Still, you need to learn the methods with which textual critics work so that, later, you can respond to such uninformed blather about the Bible, which is driven by pure hatred. That is

[1] Karlheinz Deschner, ed., *Was halten Sie vom Christentum? 18 Antworten auf eine Umfrage*, List Bücher 105 (Munich: Paul List, 1957), 64.

[2] "The great number of textual variants": This is true at least for the NT. The situation with the OT is somewhat different, since the Hebrew text is retained primarily in text-recensions prepared with the greatest care—for example, the Masoretic Text (MT). Sometime around the year 400 CE the Greek "Septuagint canon," which is more extensive than the Masoretic Text, was broadly acknowledged in the Western church as "Sacred Scripture." See Erich Zenger, et al., eds., *Einleitung in das Alte Testament*, Studienbücher Theologie 1.1 (Stuttgart: Kohlhammer, 2nd ed. 1996), 27–29.

precisely the purpose of the first part of our semester's course. So *avanti!*"

For you, my readers, let me add that over time I encountered such absolutely ignorant blather about the Bible by "offensive" atheists quite often. Apparently their hatred for Christianity is so great that they think it worthwhile to devote themselves to detailed research for their pamphlets, blogs, or letters to the editor. This striking and constantly repeated experience was once again something that strengthened my faith in God and Jesus Christ. Christian theology can withstand clear investigation and clean methodology. It has no need to cloud or distort anything, but it appears that a certain number of atheists have an urgent need for those things if they are to sustain their arguments. But back to Tübingen!

⚜

The first segment of my semester course was thus devoted to "Text," the second to "Canon." What does "canon" mean? In ancient Greek it was a tube or a staff, but the transferred meaning of the word was "measure" or "norm." That expressed something that was of signal importance for the Greeks: what was balanced, harmonic, perfect, ideal. "Canon" in this sense also described the perfected form that should be a *measure* or *standard* for everything else. In Christianity's specialized language, then, "canon" represents the "binding" rule of faith or tradition—and ultimately, since the fourth century, the official collection of Sacred Scripture. (Much later it came to be used for the unchanging part of the Eucharistic Prayer). So "Canon" in the title of my course referred to the collection of sacred writings that is used in worship: the one, normative, inviolable Holy Bible. In the lectures, obviously, the main issue was how this canon of scripture—especially that of the New Testament—came to exist in the first place.

We could certainly imagine the origins of the New Testament this way: the Great Church had twenty-seven individual writings that were *authoritative* for it and that it therefore wanted to keep together. So it bound them, so to speak, between two covers, or more precisely in a single codex, and said: "Each of these individual writings is valuable to us in itself. Therefore we have bound them together and call the whole thing 'New Testament.'" Thus the individual writings constituted a kind of small library in which the books held different—sometimes contradictory—positions, as is always the case with the books in any library. But for practical reasons the individual books were all combined in a single collective volume. As I said: we could imagine it that way. But that is *not* what happened.

At first, after Easter, Sacred Scripture consisted only of what, for centuries, and with reference to 2 Corinthians 3:14, we have called the "Old Testament." To begin with it was simply called *graphē*: "Scripture" (literally: "writing"). But the early Christian communities did not leave it at that. Even during Paul's lifetime his letters were preserved and were read aloud at worship, after the "Scripture" had first been proclaimed.

After Paul's death there was a genuine effort to collect what remained of his writings and to produce a Pauline corpus of letters. During that period the letter to the Ephesians, 2 Thessalonians, and then the Pastorals were also created. They were written by disciples of Paul, in his name and spirit, to fill the vacancy that was felt to exist in the communities he had founded, after his death. Evidently these post-Pauline letters were very quickly added to the collection of Paul's authentic letters. The result was a *Corpus Paulinum*. Readings from it were part of worship, and in that way it became "Sacred Scripture" as well.

Still, that was only part of what was later called the "New Testament," since not only Paul's letters but other writings, above all the gospels, were presented in the worship of early Christian communities. A selection was made from the whole of these writings—letters and gospels—and carefully combined to form what was then called the "New Testament." I have deliberately described all this in vague terms because the precise point in time when all that happened can no longer be determined, nor do we know anything about the persons who performed this work of composition.

Four gospels were chosen as the basis for the collection-in-process: the one we know today as Matthew's, together with those of Mark, Luke, and John. However, Luke's Gospel was structured differently from the other three. It had a continuation, a second book: the so-called Acts of the Apostles. Shaping a set of canonical gospels required separating Luke's Gospel from its second volume. The four gospels were arranged one after the other and volume two of Luke's double work was added afterward, producing the sequence of four gospels plus Acts. That, obviously, was a radical form of surgery on Luke's two-volume work.

After the Acts of the Apostles, to form the New Testament canon as we know it today, came the collections of letters that had emerged alongside the grouping of gospels: first the set of authentic and non-authentic Pauline letters and then, in particular, the collection of the so-called "catholic epistles." The name comes from the fact that these (at least James, 1 and 2 Peter, 1 John, and Jude) were not addressed to individual communities but to larger regional churches or even the church as a whole. ("Catholic" originally did not refer to a confession, but to the Great Church found throughout the Roman empire.) Ultimately the whole was rounded off with the book of Revelation.

This process yielded a well-ordered and considered composition of New Testament writings: first the gospels with the appearance of Jesus, and at the end of the whole book the return of Jesus at the end of time (Revelation). Between these we read of the gathering of the church made up of Jews and Gentiles, and Paul's letters have equal weight with those of the "pillars" of James, Peter, and John (Gal 2:9). This emphasizes the unity of the church. With reference to 2 Corinthians 3:6 the whole volume was called "New Testament."[3]

To repeat: all this should be understood as a careful process of redaction—by highly competent, believing Christians—carried out for the purpose of creating *a single homogeneous book*. The New Testament is thus not a more or less accidental collection of important early Christian writings, but a real book with a well-thought-out theological composition that reveals a clear authorial intent.

[3] The phrase is now properly translated "new covenant" at 2 Cor 3:6. "Testament" in this Pauline context comes from the AV.—Tr.

Notable in all this is that the New Testament is deliberately connected to the "Scriptures" (that is, the "Old Testament"). "Scripture" is the foundation of the whole. The New Testament was incorporated into "Scripture" and so grew together with the Old Testament to form a single, still larger book. It is, we might say, the last layer of interpretation of the Old Testament. And like the Torah (the Pentateuch) in the Old Testament, the canon of four gospels formed the basis for the New Testament.

Thus the compositional intent that underlies the New Testament and the Sacred Scriptures as a whole is unmistakable. The authors who created this organic work intended that it should be seen as a unified book. The early Christian theologian Origen was right when he wrote, in his commentary on John:

> We must approach the whole of Scripture as one body, we must not lacerate nor break through the strong and well-knit connections which exist in the harmony of its whole composition, as those do who [on their own authority] lacerate the unity of the Spirit that imbues all the Scriptures.[4]

"Authorial intent," of course, does not mean that a single theologian or bishop created the New Testament canon. It may certainly have been a collective. Moreover, the creation of the canon of the New Testament was also a lengthy process: what had been created in an act of genius had to be recognized and accepted by all the church's communities if it were really to be the canon of the whole church. Obviously that took a long time. But because that process of acceptance was necessary and actually occurred, the whole of the Great Church at that time can be called co-author or, to put it more cautiously, co-publisher of the canon.

That probably makes it clear what "canon" meant in my lecture series and what I had to present to my students, step by step, in individual classes. What has just been said about "canon" was of

[4] Origen, *Commentary on the Gospel of John* X, 13 (*Sources chrétiennes* 157, 446), *alt.*, and at https://www.newadvent.org/fathers/101510.htm. Origen is referring to the eating of the Paschal meal according to Exod 12:3-10 and interpreting the text allegorically. The translation given here is derived from Marius Reiser, *Bibelkritik und Auslegung der Heiligen Schrift. Beiträge zur Geschichte der biblischen Exegese und Hermeneutik*, WUNT 217 (Tübingen: Mohr Siebeck, 2007), 127.

extraordinary importance for a right approach to the text—that is, the "hermeneutics" of biblical texts. For if the whole canon is a single book, no individual text can be interpreted in isolation and only for its own sake. I have to read it in light of all the other relevant texts in the Bible. Let me give a concrete example, one I used in my first semester-long course and also liked to apply later in other forums:

The parable of the violent vineyard workers (Matt 21:33-46) already played a major role at an early point in the church's history as a basis for a theology of the *disinheritance and rejection of Israel*. In Mark's version of the parable Jesus says that the owner of the vineyard will come, kill the violent vintners, and give the vineyard *to others* (Mark 12:9). *Jesus meant that as a sharp warning to his opponents, not as an unchangeable fact*. Matthew took up that line in his Markan model, expanded it, and sharpened it still further. In Matthew the text now reads:

> Therefore I tell you, the reign of God will be taken away from you and given to a people that produces the expected fruits. (Matt 21:43, NRSVue alt.)

The similarity to Matthew 8:12 (where the "heirs of the kingdom" will be thrown into the outer darkness) is obvious. While the imagery is different, the statement in Matthew 21:43 points in the same direction; in fact, it seems to be even more clearly about the "disinheritance of Israel" because it says explicitly that the reign of God will be given to another "people." That can only be the church. So do we have in Matthew 21:43 a statement that legitimates later positions maintaining that Israel has been *expelled* from salvation history?

The point can be argued.[5] But even if Matthew may have seen things differently, he still formulated his statement in a way that created misunderstanding. For the moment let us assume the worst case: that the author of Matthew's Gospel really wanted to enunciate a theology of disinheritance. In that case, of course, we must hear not only *that author*'s voice, because there is another

[5] It is arguable because in the context Matthew makes it clear that this is only about the leadership group in Israel (cf. Matt 21:45).

that addresses the question—namely, that of Paul in Romans 9–11, where he asks whether Israel has been expelled from the history of salvation or whether its election by God is irrevocable. And here the voice of the letter to the Romans is weightier than all others in the New Testament because Paul posed the question explicitly, in fundamental terms, and at extended length.

In other words: if we ask in theological terms about God's enduring fidelity to God's people Israel, or about a possible rejection of Israel, the whole of the New Testament has to be heard, above all Romans 9–11 (and especially 11:29).

But more than that: the Old Testament has to be heard as well, because the question of whether God could reject this people and seek a new one is already treated thoroughly and at length in the Old Testament (above all in Exod 32:7-14). Thus the whole question can only be decided "canonically": that is, by including all of Sacred Scripture. Those are, in themselves, perfectly obvious statements but, alas, they are often forgotten—whenever Sacred Scripture is regarded not as a single book but as a collection of individual books that have nothing to do with each other. Even the early Christian theologians who argued for the unity of Scripture disregarded their own hermeneutical principles in this matter. The consequences were dreadful: centuries of persecution of Jews in the Christian West, and in the end, Auschwitz.

I wanted, by saying all that, to show not only what "Text, Canon, Hermeneutics" meant. I also wanted to emphasize the role that "Introduction to the New Testament" and "Introduction to the Old Testament" play within the framework of the canon of theological studies. Naturally there is a great deal more—especially introductions to the individual biblical writings. For example, an introduction to Paul's letter to the Romans has to answer a great many questions: when did Paul write this letter, where, for whom, and why? What is the letter's structure; what is its principal theme?

So in those first Tübingen semesters I had a lot of work to do. I had to deal with much of the material for the first time and get a good grasp on it. Still, those were good years, because my students entered into the work also. Here again, let me give an example:

I missed the climax of the student unrest in Tübingen toward the end of the 1960s. When I came there in 1973, Professor Joseph Ratzinger had already moved to Regensburg because lectures in Tübingen were continually being interrupted. I only experienced occasional fallout, but it was still disruptive. One morning my colleagues and I could not lecture in the Kupferbau because, during the night, students in revolt had sealed the doors with heavy chains. On another occasion we had to move to the auditorium in the Theology Department building (where we had "owners' rights") because of the ongoing interruptions by students from another department. A third time, a group of sociology students stormed in during my lecture and wanted to make my listeners "discuss" the "exploitation" and "alienation" of the student body and the necessity of "democratizing" the university. "Discussing," of course, meant "proclaiming" their own position. One of my students rose and said: "If you really want to democratize the university, please leave the lecture hall now, because the students sitting here all want to hear Professor Lohfink's lecture." The students' assent, in the form of the usual knuckle-rapping and stamping of feet, was so powerful and so clear that the group departed.

The three years in which I worked as a C-3 assistant professor in Tübingen went by as if they had wings. Then Professor Karl Hermann Schelkle (1908–1988), the occupant of the professorship for New Testament theology in the department, retired, and the position was declared open. Some colleagues advised me to apply—and my application was accepted by the faculty synod.

Certainly that increased my obligations. As the content of the "box from the cellar" revealed, I now held (spread out over several years) lectures on "Jesus' Message and Practice," "Narrative Structure and Theology of Jesus' Parables," "History and Theology of the Earliest Community," "Principal Themes in Pauline Theology," "Principal Themes in Johannine Theology," "Galatians," "Titus," and "Origins and Nature of Apocalypticism." Obviously all that had to be prepared, but in the process I learned a great deal—for my own faith as well. And without that preliminary work I could never have written my later books.

At this point I must by all means also mention the good work of the many students who wrote their final year projects and diploma theses under my direction. Obviously I assigned them topics that were of burning interest to me, too. Still more important for me, certainly, was the help and friendly cooperation of my assistants: first Iris Bosold, then Marius Reiser, and later the invaluable work of my American doctoral student, Dr. Linda Maloney. After her return to the United States she translated almost all my books into English and thus gained me a great many readers throughout the world. But at this point I must also mention the pleasant and collegial society of the other professors in the discipline. Once a month we were invited to the house of one of our colleagues where, over dinner and afterward, we spoke about and discussed every topic imaginable.

I have especially fond memories of a journey the whole faculty made together to Israel. But what remains most vivid to me is a very official invitation we as a faculty received from the theological faculty of the University of Budapest. It was my first trip behind the "Iron Curtain" (at that time Hungary was still under Soviet domination). My "pertinent" experiences began as soon as we set foot in the "Socialist People's Republic." Our plane had successfully landed and we now stood in a long line at passport control. The customs official was virtually invisible. He was not seated behind a glass partition or an open barrier but instead was enclosed in a gigantic wooden structure with two narrow slits: one at eye-level and another, below, where papers could be inserted. I saw almost nothing but the man's eyes. They fixed on me, then glanced down—where and for what purpose, of course, I could not see. I had no idea what the man was actually doing. Then he again looked at me with piercing eyes and sank his glance again. This process was repeated several times before he finally shoved my passport back at me without a single word. I found the whole thing spooky, and I remembered an adage: that you can recognize the character of a government from how you are treated at the border.

We went directly from the airport to a hotel and thence to an official reception by the Faculty of Theology. It followed the customary ritual: speeches of greeting, introductions, buffet, bland conversation, information about the program for the coming days. Everything was extremely polite and correct—but at the same time there was a peculiar distance I could not interpret. It could not be because of language differences, since many of our hosts spoke German, and English was an aid to the rest.

It was only in the evening that we got an explanation for this cautious reserve. The dean had spoken privately with some of us as individuals and invited us to his home. Actually, we *all* were there; two of the Hungarian professors, however, were absent. The dean explained to us that those two were spies the government had inserted into the faculty, and they knew nothing about this private meeting. The evening then proceeded altogether differently than had the previous reception: that is, with open conversations, a lot of laughter, and the warmth one constantly encounters in Hungary.

In the winter semester of 1978/1979 I was elected dean, and after that it was unavoidable that my parents and I would have to move, because as dean I had to be present in Tübingen both morning and afternoon. Since the drive from Öschelbronn to Tübingen took half an hour, that meant two lost hours every day. I could not afford that. So I sought another dwelling for us, as close to Tübingen as possible. I bought a house in Wurmlingen, directly below the Kapellenberg (Chapel Hill) that Ludwig Uhland had celebrated in verse ("There above stands the chapel"). A favorable interest rate made the financing possible.

Now my parents finally had a house of their own, something they had dreamed of for many years. There was enough space for a long patio and a big garden right next to the house. To the disgust of the previous owner, my father immediately dug up his "sacred lawn" and sowed lamb's lettuce (field salad), even though it was fall. I planted four apple trees, two cherry trees, and two plum trees close to the house, and very soon a vine stretched its branches over the patio, like the one that had shaded our dwelling in the *Kuhwaldsiedlung* in Frankfurt. My parents were happy. So was I: above all because I could now be at the theology building in Tübingen in ten minutes.

Another of the many happy memories of my time in Tübingen is Sunday worship. Öschelbronn was an old village, but after the war it had been enlarged to include a new section, and there, in the heart of a purely Lutheran space, were new settlers, almost all of them people who had been expelled from Silesia, and mainly Roman Catholics. At the center of the settlement a new church had been built: not very large, and quite homey. Immediately after moving to Öschelbronn I had agreed with the diocese of Rottenburg-Stuttgart that I would regularly celebrate Sunday Mass there. That continued even after I later moved closer to Tübingen.

Those Sunday services brought me profound joy, and not only because of the fidelity of the exiles. Rather, I very quickly developed a cordial relationship with the Lutheran pastor in Öschelbronn. We exchanged pulpits from time to time: he would preach at one of my Sunday services or I at one of his. In this way I became acquainted with a considerable number of the members of the Lutheran parish—and with them, for the first time in my life, with Swabian Pietism.

I am still grateful for this acquaintance. These people I now met, some of whom became true friends, were deeply believing Christians. They gathered with many others from their community every Sunday afternoon for a so-called "Hour" in which, quite independently of their pastor, they read aloud from Scripture and prayed together. But not only that: they rendered mutual aid when one of them was in need, and some of them made a road trip at least once a year to the DDR (East Germany). They smuggled in carefully concealed Bibles and foodstuffs.

The Swabian Pietism I thus encountered had its own language. At Christmas people wished me "much blessed time," and I received New Year's greetings that read: "We wish you soundness of body, peace of soul, and the Holy Spirit." In a truly ecumenical spirit my new friends even attended my worship services from time to time—and then it could happen that afterward one of them would say to me: "Professor, sir, I have noticed that you love our Lord Jesus as we do."

Some of these new acquaintances also made friends with my parents. In summer they brought us fruits and vegetables and, if we invited them to stay, they told us wonderful stories. For example, a somewhat elderly couple told how they met when they were young. They both worked at Daimler; in the mornings they were collected by the factory bus, along with a lot of others from their several villages, and late in the afternoon they were brought back. So they saw each other every day. HE thought: "That is certainly a sweet, pious girl. She would be the right one for me." SHE thought: "That is surely a trustworthy, believing man. He would be the right one for me." But they did not dare to speak to each other. Each of them prayed to the Holy Spirit for insight. At some point they did, after all, begin to converse: they told each other how they had prayed month after month; they agreed on a period of waiting and still more prayer; then they became engaged, married, and they said, with mischievous laughter: "We still love each other—and in fact, more and more every year."

I know: there was also another side to this deep and endearing faith. Thus in Tübingen before every Carnival season there raged in the local papers, in the letters to the editor, an unending strife over whether the kindergarteners should be allowed to wear masks, or whether that should be forbidden on the ground of decency and good morals. And when, during that season, I traveled south to the "Oberland" to give a lecture I could see at a glance, in every village I drove through, whether it was Catholic or Lutheran. The Lutheran villages had only *one* pub, and during Carnival everything was grey and quiet. In the Catholic villages there were at least an old tavern and a new pub, often also in mountainous areas an upper tavern and a lower tavern. And the village streets were spanned by lines from which hung stockings, underpants, and brassieres, while a colorful Carnival celebration went on below.

Once I had an unforgettable "encounter." This was after we had moved to Wurmlingen. An official had come to test my heating system. I went with him into the basement and we soon entered into conversation: he asked what I did for a living and, when I told him, immediately began to examine me on the subject of the New Testament. Finally I said that his extreme fundamentalism was rather a hindrance to a right interpretation. When he had finished checking the heating and was leaving, he turned back again and said threateningly: "Trust me! You are damned!" That was something else one might encounter in Baden-Württemberg, but I do not believe it had anything to do with Swabian Pietism, which I experienced very differently: in its best and most reasonable form also in professors in the Lutheran Faculty of Theology at the university. They were all scholars with whom I had been long acquainted through professional literature and whom I now met on many occasions, and they included, above all, Martin Hengel, Hartmut Gese, Peter Stuhlmacher, Otfried Hofius, and Otto Betz. We saw each other often in the theology building or in the Kupferbau, but above all at the regular meetings of the Lutheran and Roman Catholic biblical scholars at which each professor in turn gave a lecture that was then intensively discussed.

I owe a great deal to those meetings. Above all, I noticed that in individual conversations with those mentioned above I often moved on to questions of faith through which we then advanced relatively quickly to personal credal affirmations. I experienced that as very refreshing and a help to forging connections. Peter Stuhlmacher once organized a common seminar with me—and from then on, until today, we have remained in friendly, collegial contact.

On the whole I also learned a great deal to the benefit of my own faith in God while I was in Tübingen—not only through the new friends in faith I met there; not only through the encounter with the Bible-believing Swabian Pietists; not only from my Silesian "Sunday parishioners" in Öschelbronn; not only through the many students who came to me during office hours and with whom I often entered into very personal conversations. Rather, it was also through my own continued study of Sacred Scripture that is the basis for my profession and that went on without interruption. Now I absolutely must say something about the basic tendency of that "continuing study" before I close the chapter on Tübingen.

At the beginning of the 1980s, Bishop Georg Moser had invited me to give a lecture for all the priests and deacons of the diocese in the cathedral at Rottenburg. I suggested as the topic: "The Idea of Community: Jesus and the Early Church." Two things had brought me to this formulation of the theme: first, reading Adolf von Harnack's book, *Das Wesen des Christentums*,[6] and then also the news of a "church mobile unit" in Berlin. Both of them had

[6] Adolf von Harnack, *What is Christianity? Sixteen Lectures*, trans. Thomas Bailey Saunders (New York: G. P. Putnam's Sons, 1901).

excited and annoyed me, and they shaped the beginning of my lecture.

Adolf von Harnack (1851–1930) was one of the most influential Protestant theologians in Germany at the beginning of the twentieth century. He represented a theological trend of the late nineteenth century that he himself called "religious individualism" and "subjectivism." He was able to use both concepts, without a shadow of criticism, in the book just mentioned. He was convinced that those ideas correctly and appropriately described Jesus' preaching as well.[7] So he wrote, in *What is Christianity?*, the since-famous and often-quoted words:

> If anyone wants to know what the kingdom of God and the coming of it meant in Jesus' message, he must read and study his parables. He will then see what it is that is meant. The kingdom of God comes by coming to the individual, by entering into his soul and laying hold of it. True, the kingdom of God is the rule of God; but it is the rule of the holy God in the hearts of individuals; *it is God himself in his power*. From this point of view everything that was dramatic in the external and historical sense has vanished; and gone, too, are all the external hopes for the future. Take whatever parable you will, the parable of the sower, of the pearl of great price, of the treasure buried in the field—the word of God, God himself, is the kingdom. It is not a question of angels and devils, thrones and principalities, but of God and the soul, the soul and its God.[8]

Thus, according to Harnack, the reign of God by no means happens in the world, in a people, in a community; it happens only in the hearts of many individuals.

> . . . the individual is called upon to listen to the glad message of mercy and the Fatherhood of God, and to make up his mind whether he will be on God's side and the Eternal's, or on the side of the world and of time.[9]

[7] Harnack, *What is Christianity?*, 25–26.
[8] Harnack, *What is Christianity?*, 33.
[9] Harnack, *What is Christianity?*, 73.

Thus, just as the reign of God happens not in a community but only within the individual, so also it has nothing to do with what is external but only with what is internal, the inner person, the soul. In fact, "the individual" and "the internal" are keywords that repeatedly occur in Harnack's writing.

Now certainly Harnack knew the New Testament much too well for him to have overlooked the idea of community that appears there as part of the Gospel of the reign of God. He wrote that the Jesus movement, after the break with the Jewish people, regarded itself as "church," meaning by that "the true Israel."[10] So Harnack was by no means on the side of those for whom the church, by its nature, must be something purely internal and therefore invisible.[11]

But in the end the extreme individualism of Harnack's theology obscured all those insights. The church is then ultimately nothing but a "community of brothers" including all well-meaning people throughout the world.[12] No matter how much Harnack asserted that the church is visible insofar as it must repeatedly make itself concrete in socially visible groups—ultimately it remains for him a purely spiritual community, a *societas in cordibus* that cannot be identified with any of the concrete churches of its time. For him that meant rejection of the Old Testament and an anti-Judaism that misconstrued the very essence of Torah.

The following is decisive: Harnack was by no means alone in his individualistic image of church and redemption; rather, he is representative of a broad current of liberal theology at the end of the nineteenth and beginning of the twentieth centuries. Also, it may well be that the Roman Catholic Church, while it held fast to concepts, formulae, and institutions that were at first shaped by an intensive idea of community, gradually came to interpret and live those concepts, formulae, and institutions in a way that was much more individualistic than their original meaning. There is good evidence that Roman Catholic theology and piety partici-

[10] Harnack, *What is Christianity?*, 90.

[11] This was especially well developed by Karl H. Neufeld, *Adolf von Harnacks Konflikt mit der Kirche. Weg-Stationen zum "Wesen des Christentums,"* Innsbrucker theologische Studien 4 (Innsbruck: Tyrolia, 1979).

[12] Harnack, *What is Christianity?*, 104–6, 137.

pated much more intensively in the forms of modern individualism than the church itself suspected. And it could be that such individualism shaped our concepts of pastoral care, our ideas about church, and the concrete constitution of our parishes much more powerfully than we would like to believe.

That brings me to the second thing that had so annoyed me: the news story about the institution of a church mobile unit in Berlin: more precisely, a vehicle equipped with short-wave radio in which a priest, a physician, and a psychologist were on call, day and night. That sounded highly modern: the church on the front lines, so to speak, or modern technology in service for the reign of God! In reality that church mobile unit was a highly questionable symbol of what the church has become in our society, by and large: a caretaker for individuals: an institution that makes "free offers" to a group of them.

That is precisely the situation of our consumer society, which Gisbert Greshake once compared to a big shopping center: every person goes around with her or his shopping cart and chooses what is attractive and what one has need of.[13] In the gigantic "Constitutional Republic Shopping Mall" there is, among many other things, a corner where "religious offerings" are on display for individuals. That is what churches are for. The society certainly wants that corner to be occupied; after all, there should be a complete supply of goods on display.—To me this mobile religious strike force seems like a perfect symbol of a consoling, caring, consumer church that leaves people in a state of isolation.

We really should not accept as inevitable and simply a matter of course the ways in which ministry is performed, at present, in many (not all) parishes and groups of parishes. And Roman Catholic Christians should not be too confident that the question of community is not at all a problem for them because their church has always held fast to the idea of community—the concept of visible, tangible *communitas*. Certainly it is true that "church" means concrete, identifiable belonging-together, a togetherness

[13] Gisbert Greshake, "Einige Überlegungen zu den Ursachen des mangelden Priesternachwuchses," in *Priesterliche Existenz heute – Sorge um geistliche Berufe*, Handreichungen zur Pastoral (Vienna: Pastoralamt d. Erzdiözese Wien, 1980), 5–19, at 8–9.

that is a vehicle of salvation.[14] The Roman Catholic Church has never denied that, nor has it really forgotten it. But the question is whether in this regard it is not undermining its own traditions and losing sight of them to a much greater degree than it realizes.

The problem indicated here was not resolved even after Vatican II. It is true that the conciliar texts, above all the Constitution on the Church (*Lumen Gentium*), gave a magnificent presentation of the community aspect. The council speaks of the church as the "community of faith, hope, and charity," as a "visible assembly," as the "messianic people of God," the "source of unity," and above all it says that "it pleased God to bring [humanity] together as one people, a people that acknowledges [God] in truth and serves [God] in holiness."[15]

These are precious words. They recall much of what the early church knew and lived—and even so, the church's reality is still far removed from such beautiful words and phrases. The council's statements feel more like consolations or promises in a dry land that cries out for rain.

Is there such a thing as community among us in a normal Sunday worship service? The person who sits nearby in the pew is a stranger to me; I don't even know her name. I know nothing of this neighbor's joys and sorrows, needs and satisfactions. But if I do know who he is and what is his name, he conceals his neediness from me, and I myself hide my own concerns from him. Certainly we shake hands at the eucharistic greeting of peace, maybe even smile at one another: but is that "community of faith, hope, and love"? Is it what Paul means when he writes to the community in Philippi:

> Only, live your life in a manner worthy of the gospel of Christ. . . . Make my joy complete: be of the same mind, having the same love, being in full accord and of one mind. Do nothing from selfish ambition or empty conceit, but in humility regard others as better than yourselves. Let each of

[14] Cf. the groundbreaking work of Henri de Lubac, *Catholicisme. Les aspects sociaux du dogme* (Paris: Cerf, 1938). English: *Catholicism: Christ and the Common Destiny of Man*, trans. Lancelot C. Sheppard (San Francisco: Ignatius, 1988).

[15] *LG* I, 8; II, 9.

> you look not to your own interests but to the interests of others. (Phil 1:27; 2:2-4)

There are many other texts like this in Paul's writings, but such instruction presupposes a close communal relationship in the group, a being-joined-together beyond the assembly for worship. And what did Jesus think about community? Did he really just relate to individuals? Was Harnack right when he repeatedly said that Jesus' concern was only with God and the soul, the soul and its God?

Those were the observations and thoughts that drove me when I suggested to Bishop Moser that my title for the lecture he proposed should be: "The Idea of Community: Jesus and the Early Church." My talk then began with the concerns sketched out above and sought to answer them.

Later, when my brother read the manuscript of the lecture, he advised me to turn it into a book. I liked the suggestion, but I couldn't begin to think about it during the semester or even in the so-called "free time between semesters," because then the classes for the next semester had to be prepared—to say nothing of taking care of the daily necessities of life.

All that remained was my personal vacation. So in the following summer I drove my car, filled with books, to Austria. There I rented a vacation cottage, worked intensively on the book every forenoon, and took long hikes in the afternoons. I made good progress with my project, and what was still lacking I could finish after vacation with the aid of my assistants.

The book was published by Herder in 1982 under the title *Wie hat Jesus Gemeinde gewollt? Zur gesellschaftlichen Dimension des christlichen Glaubens*.[16] It sold a great many copies and was translated in the United States, France, Italy, Spain, Brazil, Hungary, Tanzania, and South Korea. Evidently I had hit a nerve.

[16] Literally: *What Kind of Community Did Jesus Want? On the Social Dimension of Christian Faith*. The American edition, translated by John P. Galvin (Philadelphia: Fortress, 1984), bore the less-specific title *Jesus and Community*, with the same subtitle. A thoroughly revised and updated new edition was published by the Katholisches Bibelwerk in 2015, with the subtitle "Kirche im Kontrast" ("Church in Contrast").

I have described all this in such detail here because in my last years in Tübingen the theme of church/people of God/community occupied my thoughts more and more. I published some other essays, conducted a seminar on the theme of "House Churches in the New Testament," and even participated in a small "house community" in Rottenburg. The first names of its members can be found in the dedication of the 1982 book. My voluntary departure from university service in the year 1986 cannot be understood apart from the theological background I have described.

It happened this way: over the years I had heard several times about a Roman Catholic community called *Die Integrierte Gemeinde* (The Integrated Community). I also knew that the New Testament scholar Rudolf Pesch had resigned his professorship at the University of Freiburg in order to live and work there. We happened to meet at a gathering of New Testament scholars, and he invited me to visit the community, whose central location was in Munich.

I accepted, and at some point I traveled to Munich for a weekend. There I was invited to participate in a gathering of the community on Saturday and in the Sunday worship service. I scarcely remember the details, but I do recall how impressed I was by the number and variety of people I met there: Germans and Swiss, Austrians and Italians, old and young, with all sorts of different personalities, and the greatest variety of jobs—cooks and merchants, artisans and artists, doctors, teachers, and scholars. Some of them lived in large houses they had purchased or rented and in which they shared meals but had their own private apartments. Others lived privately but had connections to the larger houses.

I learned that they met every Saturday afternoon and evening—and I experienced it myself. The purpose of the gathering was to prepare in detail for the next day's worship. Texts were distributed to readers and songs were rehearsed. More important, certainly, was a careful introduction to the readings for the next day, from the Old and New Testaments and the Gospel, led by one of the community's theologians. But there was something else that was altogether unfamiliar to me: namely, a look back at what had happened in the community during the previous week, together with a review of current events in the world and society. The celebration of Mass then followed on Sunday, and of course its lively character was due to the previous day's preparations. Everything was thought-through, meaningful, and carried out with the participation of everyone—something I had never before experienced.

I visited a second time, then a third time, and at some point I also joined a celebration of Holy Week and the Easter Vigil. My first Easter night in the community is something I can never forget. In the forenoon of Holy Saturday we prepared thoroughly for the night service and Easter morning. The common preparation was itself a part of the feast. Then, in the afternoon, we all rested and slept. When night came we met again and sat together in a big circle. All the lessons appointed for the liturgy from the Old Testament (as well as those from the New) were presented—not just at full length, but often with an expanded text. And the texts were not just read aloud: the speakers had learned them by heart and presented them in the proper spirit and with full engagement. Between the readings there were brief explanations of the next text to be presented, together with sung psalms augmented by new antiphons created in the community. The "Song at the Sea" about Israel's rescue from Pharaoh's army (Exod 15:1-21) was not just sung; all those present joined in a circle dance while singing. At some point before that we had eaten a brief snack, taken while standing—recalling how the Israelites ate before their departure from Egypt. The night passed more rapidly than I had expected. By the time we lighted the Easter fire and, from it, the paschal candle, morning was already dawning and the first blackbirds were singing. Then, as we celebrated the Easter Mass, the sun had arisen. Our celebration was followed by a long Easter breakfast, and then we all went home to sleep.

This feast made clear to me, in a new way, what liturgy can be and what power it possesses when God's saving deeds are truly remembered and celebrated. As I was driving home to Tübingen, through Ulm and over the Swabian Alp, I found I was softly singing the hymn "Holy God, We Praise Thy Name." I had spoken so often in my lectures about the "people of God" and what "community" is, almost entirely as pure theory. Now I had lived it.

The leaders of the community made an agreement with me that I would travel to Munich once a month so that I could share in the community's life at least to that extent. At some point, then,

I was in a community gathering—I think it was in the affiliated community in Hagen in Westphalia—and I was asked whether I did not want to join the community fully. Then everything happened again as it had when I decided to become a priest: there was my resistance, there were my fears, my attempts to avoid the question, and then a new life-decision—and finally the profound, silent joy, once I had decided.

However, this time the external circumstances were somewhat more difficult. It was not just a matter of leaving the house in Wurmlingen, which had become such a joy; it was also about my parents. Should I settle them in a retirement home? I did not want to do that. But I most certainly did not want to put pressure on them to accompany me. To enable them to choose freely I took them with me to Munich and showed them the "Integrated House" where we would live together, with the Lohfink family in one section. A little after that they decided to go with me. In this case—differently from other times in his marriage—it was my father who set things in motion. One night he dreamed that he was once again driving his Trans-Europa Express, and all the signals showed that the tracks were open.

After that, everything moved very quickly. First I asked permission from my then-bishop in Limburg, Franz Kamphaus, and then I informed Georg Moser, bishop of Rottenburg-Stuttgart. Next came the faculty, and after that the president of the university, Adolf Theis. Again I sat, as I had thirteen years previously, in his outer office—and this time he tried to induce me to stay. But the die was cast, and the move went smoothly.

Still, I had to continue my duties for two semesters, until the position was advertised and a successor—it was to be Michael Theobald—could assume the professorship. During that time I lived in the seminary in Tübingen. Shortly before my final departure I gave my farewell lecture.[17] Its subject was "The Crisis of Exegesis over Jesus' Proclamation of the Reign of God," and it began as follows:

[17] The entire farewell lecture can be found under the title "Die Not der Exegese mit der Reich-Gottes-Verkündigung Jesu" in Gerhard Lohfink, *Studien zum Neuen Testament*, SBA 5 (Stuttgart: KBW, 1989), 383–402.

A farewell lecture is, besides what may be said about theology, the place to give thanks for many things. First and foremost I thank the Faculty of Catholic Theology for calling me to Tübingen fourteen years ago—to join a faculty that is an indispensable part of the history of Catholic theology. No matter how punctilious the hiring process is, in the end a faculty must always perform a radical act of trust, and that trust I experienced here. It was echoed for me again [this evening] in Dean Peter Hünermann's introduction. Here I found a broad field for research, a space of freedom without financial anxieties, where I could teach and publish—the latter in the world's oldest still-existing theological periodical, the *Theologische Quartalschrift*.[18] Freedom to study, teach, and publish—that sounds quite normal, but if one looks around the world and throughout history one sees immediately how far from normal it is. The Faculty of Catholic Theology also afforded me constant opportunity to speak with dear and valued colleagues from whom I could always learn something. I would have loved to attend at least one lecture given by most of them, but I never dared to.

My thanks also to all my acquaintances and friends in the Faculty of Lutheran Theology. They not only expanded my theological world; I was able, again and again, to engage in very personal, even spiritual conversations about the Bible that strengthened my faith. As much as the existence alongside one another of two theological faculties is a real symbol of a dreadful wound in the church—namely, its division—so much so was this neighborly relationship a profound enrichment and constant stimulation for me.

I also thank the many students who listened to my lectures here in the Kupferbau during the last fourteen years. At first I always entered the lecture hall with fear and trembling: would anyone even listen to me? Dear students: that you did listen, that you came again and again, and that I was able to learn from your openness and love for truth while your youthfulness invigorated me—what a gift that has been!

There is much more that could be said and many thanks to be given, but most of it must remain unspoken. One thing,

[18] *Theological Quarterly*, founded 1819.

however, I can say: a German theological faculty is not merely a public institution; it also teaches on behalf of the church. Here I want to express explicitly my gratitude for the trust continually placed in me by Bishop Georg Moser, his colleagues in ministry, and the whole diocese of Rottenburg-Stuttgart. In the past fourteen years I have never experienced any interference in my research and teaching. Instead I have found community in faith, concern for the Gospel, Swabian rationality, and a humanity that has repeatedly shattered every threat that the church might become a bureaucratic system like the rest of society.

If I am now departing it is not because I did not find a home in this local church or could no longer endure the business of the university. Nor is it because, as one concerned colleague wrote to me, I am experiencing a midlife crisis. It is because I have stumbled upon something that is more powerful and fascinating than anything I have experienced before. But because it is difficult to speak of love within the limits of a lecture, I will now talk about the objective foundation of this thing—namely, the reign of God. . . .

11

Community

As we have just heard, it is difficult to talk "about one's love" in a lecture—and basically, the same is true of a book! If, even so, I dare in this chapter to say more about the *Integrierte Gemeinde* it will not be in the usual manner of those who write autobiographies. Thus I will not relate my duties in the community and all that I experienced there, which would require a separate book. Instead I will pursue the underlying theological question of the "people of God" and "community" that was already mentioned in the previous chapter. There is no other way to make clear what the *Integrierte Gemeinde* was really all about, and still is—and what ultimately drew me to it. So I ask my readers to accompany me on a rather long pilgrimage—not "through the institutions" but through the history of Israel and the church. It will quickly become clear what that has to do with this new and last part of my life.

When the Old Testament talks about God's self-disclosure—that is, divine revelation—it is always about the fact that *God creates a people in the world, a people who are God's own*. In the Old Testament God's self-disclosure never involves opening the meaning, the "depths of the Godhead" in the Gnostic sense. The "depths of God" (1 Cor 2:10) are God's hidden plan for salvation. The purpose of revelation is always that God may gain a people in the world that differs from the other nations. That self-differentiation is meant to make clear what God's plan for the world is. Therefore we could say that Israel is to become a blessing for all peoples (Gen 12:3) so that, in that blessing, the nature of the true God is opened to all of them.

This is especially clear in the story of the burning bush in Exodus 3–4, where Moses receives a revelation of God. Moses asks God for the divine name, because he has to legitimate himself to the Israelites by stating the name of the god who has appeared to him. With this question Moses is still fully within the scope of ancient Near Eastern religions, in which every god and goddess had a name and, with it, his or her own "sphere of responsibility." For example, there were gods of war, of peace, of the family, of fecundity, of weather—or of sovereignty over all other gods.

But God does not give Moses a name; instead, God tells him: "I will be who I will be" (Exod 3:14). This response amounts to a refusal to give a name. The Israelites will only recognize *who God really is* in the fact that this God will rescue them from the house of slavery in Egypt and, at Sinai, will give them an alternative social order that is different from those of other nations.

Then all Israel, women and men, gathers at Sinai in order to receive this new social order: namely, Torah, which is part of the covenant. That covenant with God makes Israel "the people of God." The book of Deuteronomy names that day at Sinai the "day of assembly" = *hēmera ẻkklēsias* (Deut 9:10).

We must keep in mind that what is *truly decisive* for Israel's being-a-people is not biological descent or territory[1] or a central government, but the covenant offered to it and to which all Israel freely assents on the "day of assembly" (Exod 24:7; cf. Deut 26:17-19). According to Deuteronomy 31:10-13 this "day of assembly" is to be repeated every seventh year—always at the Feast of Booths, accompanied by the reading aloud of the whole Torah. In this way Israel is placed in its original situation every seventh year and is to learn ever anew why it is here and what its way of life

[1] Please do not apply this statement to the present-day state of Israel, which is not simply identical with what the Old Testament means by the people of God. The state of Israel is in the first place a political entity, a place of refuge for Jews who have had to flee from many lands where they have been persecuted.

is. The regular "assembly" of the people of God that was later to be so important to the church as its basic model is laid down here. The original theological location of the concept of *ekklēsia* (the church's assembly) is thus Sinai.

But Israel not only gathers every seventh year for the reading of its social contract. It also comes together annually in Jerusalem for the three great feasts: Passover, the Feast of Weeks, and the Feast of Booths. Women, men, children, enslaved persons male and female, everyone from woodworkers to water-carriers, and even foreigners are to assemble (Deut 16:11, 13-15; cf. 29:9-10). Israel lives, as it were, *from feast to feast*. That all the people then come together in one place is a real symbol of the unity and solid community within the people of God.

But what did that togetherness look like in daily life? In the ancient Near East the extended family played a crucial role. It protected individuals, furnishing them with solidarity and support. In Torah, to begin with, the ancient Near Eastern family structures were maintained but the solidarity within the family was extended to include all Israel. That is precisely what is meant by the command in Leviticus 19:18: "You shall love your neighbor as yourself." That "yourself" is not, as asserted nowadays in countless sermons, the individual "I," which one should care for in order to be able to love others. Instead, it is a collective. It is one's own family. And the "neighbors" are not just any "fellow human beings" but the members of the people of God. The command to love the neighbor in Leviticus 19 thus means: one must show the same solidarity to all those who belong to the people of God as one shows to members of one's own extended family. Moreover, that solidarity must extend even to "strangers" or "foreigners" within the people of God (Lev 19:33-34).

Jesus adopted this commandment to love the neighbor—that is, to extend family solidarity to the whole people of God as a matter of course—from Leviticus 19, and he linked it to the principal commandment to love God in Deuteronomy 6:5 (see Mark 12:29-31). All that was new was the clarity of the combination. Likewise new was that Jesus specifically and explicitly mentioned love of enemies. Indeed, love of enemies (at first within the people of God) was already included in Leviticus 19:17-18, and most certainly in Exodus 23:4-5, where it is said that one should help one's enemy if that person's donkey collapses under its burden. That is nothing other than love of enemies, because in the Bible "love" does not refer to emotions but to practical action.

Likewise a matter of course for Jesus was the institution of regular assemblies of the people of God. He himself regularly went up to Jerusalem for Israel's feasts. Certainly he gave a radical eschatological meaning to this gathering of Israel: now, since the reign of God is dawning, God "gathers" God's people definitively. Jesus says: "Whoever does not gather with me [now, in this eschatological hour] scatters" (Matt 12:30). And in the Our Father he has his disciples pray explicitly for the "gathering" of Israel in the first petition. "Hallowed be Thy Name" means first and above all: "gather, unite, and heal your people Israel, so that your Name may be hallowed" (cf. Ezek 36:22-28).

Jesus instituted a strategy for this eschatological coming-together of Israel that he had learned from the prophets: he gathers people who follow him, building a circle of disciples around himself. The primary model is Elijah's calling of Elisha as told in 1 Kings 19:19-21. From that circle of disciples Jesus chose twelve men (Mark 3:14) and sent them out two by two (Mark 6:7) to act as *official* witnesses proclaiming the now-dawning reign of God in Israel, and to expel demons and heal the sick as a sign of that inbreaking reign of God (Luke 9:1-2).

Still—and this is important in our context—the task of the Twelve was not exhausted by that mission. Mark 3:14 says explicitly that they were to be "with Jesus." Apart from their apostolic "journey" (from which they quickly return) they are thus to be constantly with Jesus—naturally not as a kind of "court," but as the realization of the new *community* in the reign of God.

Beyond the Twelve there must have been a larger group of disciples (Luke 6:17) who accompanied Jesus at least part of the time (Luke 8:1-3). Together with Jesus and the Twelve they likewise constituted the growth center for the eschatological Israel that was to be gathered. According to the gospels—this is evident especially from Mark—there was thus not only a *missio apostolica* (an "apostolic mission") but also a *vita apostolica* (an "apostolic life"). Both are necessary, and the two must mutually enhance one another.

Longing for the New Testament type of apostolic life would play an important role in the church's history. Especially in the Middle Ages that idea would become the program of many movements for church renewal.

The gospels, especially Mark's, even give more space to apostolic life than to apostolic mission. This is concretely evident in the way themes are arranged in the Markan Gospel: in it (but not only there) the conflicts within the circle of disciples and the corresponding instruction play an extraordinarily large part. More than that: many sayings of Jesus that the gospels now direct to the crowds were originally words spoken to the disciples.

An important theme of that instruction for disciples (and thus the program for apostolic life) is the demand to leave everything, even one's own family, in order to live fully and undividedly for the service of the gospel. It appears again and again in many variations (see esp. Matt 19:29). The historical context is the instances of disciples being called to follow Jesus and their unprogrammed traveling about in Galilee with him. The idea of being ready to leave everything is also connected with that of "doing without property" (see esp. Mark 10:17-31). This does not mean that ownership is something bad in itself but that it can, and often does, get in the way of the "wholeness" of surrender to the reign of God.

Another topic in the instruction for apostolic life is Jesus' appeal against the elementary force of lust for power, of the search for recognition, reputation, and influence. The disciples are not to build themselves up, but instead are to serve one another (see esp. Mark 10:35-45).

How much all those topics related to problems within the group of disciples is shown also by the demand to forgive one another without limit (Luke 11:4). Jesus radicalizes the subject of forgiveness with the example of someone who interrupts a sacrifice in the temple in order to be reconciled with a fellow believer before making the offering. The example even leaves open the question of which party is guilty. Reconciliation with the brother or sister within the people of God is the precondition for all liturgy, and it must take place immediately (Matt 5:23-24).

The theology of the cross is also part of the constant formation of the circle of disciples. Jesus probably did not first develop it when he was on the way to his death-Passover in Jerusalem (Mark 8:31-38).

Finally, decisive for instruction in apostolic life is the theme of unconditional trust in the care and protection of the Father in heaven (Matt 6:25-34). It also shapes the Our Father, which was originally a disciples' prayer. The theme of "trust" appears in the Our Father not only in the address, "*Abba*," but especially in the fourth petition (Matt 6:11//Luke 11:3). The request for bread for the day to come is proper to disciples who are traveling through Israel and do not know in the morning whether, when evening comes, anyone will receive them and give them food and lodging. (The "day to come" in the Jewish time scheme begins with the previous evening.) So much for Jesus and his instructions for his group of disciples!

Evidently the young community that reassembled in Jerusalem after Good Friday lived in terms of these instructions from Jesus and of their own experiences in the pre-Easter group of disciples. At first those who had followed Jesus ran away, but then they regathered in Jerusalem. They joined their lives with those of the others—not only because of the appearances of the Risen One but also under pressure from the Jewish society around them. Hence it is not permissible to see the summaries in Acts (esp. Acts 2:43-47 and 4:32-37) simply as utopia or whitewashing. The accusation that this is all utopian is also inappropriate because Luke certainly speaks of serious conflicts in the Jerusalem community. Consider only the betrayal by Ananias and Sapphira (Acts 5:1-11), the neglect of the widows from the Greek-speaking part of the community (Acts 6:1), and the quarrels over the circumcision of Gentile Christian men (Acts 15:1-7).

In the context of those conflicts Luke shows, using the "apostolic council" as an example, how solutions can be arrived at: the whole community gathers around the apostles and elders (Acts 15:22); God's actions in the immediate past are narrated and interpreted (Acts 15:7-12); the current event is measured against the statements of Scripture (Acts 15:13-21).

Luke also confronts Christians in his own time (and thus, of course, ourselves) with what had proved within a few decades to be the enduring structure of the church as the eschatologically gathered (and further *to be* gathered) Israel—above all, also, in the context of confrontations with Gnostic heretics (the great danger to the church I spoke of above in Chapter 9). The intent is to show what church is, and Luke does so primarily by repeatedly picturing the gatherings of the Jerusalem community.

According to the first chapter of Acts that community assembled regularly, not only for prayer but also for discussion of their common problems. In doing so they strove for unanimity (Acts 1:14; 4:24; 15:25)—conscious, however, that it was the work of the Holy Spirit. They gathered again and again for common meals "with glad and generous hearts" (Acts 2:46) because they found that the Risen One was in their midst. But the community not only shared meals: they shared their lives with one another. For example, they tried to achieve what Torah prescribes: a constant equalization between poor and rich (Acts 4:32-37).

This community was a visible gathering around the twelve apostles, as shown by Acts 1:15, which numbers the group at 120. It is an assembly in which each knows about the sorrows and joys, the cares and delights of the others. How could it be possible to share responsibility for the faith of others in a mega-community?

However, the basic plan of this primeval picture of the church is not just the group, even though *ẻkklēsia* simply means "gathering" or "assembly." There are countless gatherings in the world. The full existence of the church happens only in the kind of assembly that is entirely a listening appeal, asking for the coming of the Spirit (Acts 1:14), because it knows that it is completely incapable of creating anything like a community by its own efforts: that would end in inescapable rivalries. *In all this Luke very carefully paints a picture of what, based on its origins, church must be.*

Certainly this image that Luke paints leaves a great deal open. New problems arose in the communities around the Mediterranean with their port cities and the accompanying mobility and multitude of private cults. Paul had to apply himself to those issues. "Encouragement (or: admonishment, *paraklēsis*)" occupies a good deal of space in his letters. A great deal could be said about that, but I can only mention a few things. It will appear that the idea of the "community" in Paul's thought, just as in that of Luke, is the inescapable and fundamental basis of Christian life.

For example, Paul speaks about the "*ekklēsia* of God that is in Corinth" (1 Cor 1:2; 2 Cor 1:1) in order to say that the eschatological community of salvation created by God that began in Jerusalem and spread to many other places also has a "presence" in Corinth (and so also in other Christian communities). When currently some theologians speak in almost triumphal tones of the "collapse of community theology" they are worlds apart from the intent of the New Testament, and in fact from the whole Bible.

For Paul, just as for Luke, the joining of Christians' real lives plays a crucial role. That joining appears in his language in the frequency of the reciprocal "together" and "with one another." We find these phrases repeatedly in the genuine Pauline letters. To give just a few examples: "love one another with mutual affection" (Rom 12:10); "be of one mind with one another" (Rom 12:16); "live in harmony with one another" (Rom 12:16); "welcome one another" (Rom 15:7); "instruct [or: admonish] one another" (Rom 15:14); "wait for one another" at the eucharistic meal (1 Cor 11:33); "have the same care for one another" (1 Cor 12:25); "through love become slaves to one another" (Gal 5:13);[2] "bear one another's burdens" (Gal 6:2); "encourage one another" (1 Thess 5:11).

Mutual correction in particular falls within these instructions. Correcting one another in love and humbly receiving the correction calls for a high degree of Christian discipleship and a corresponding *ethos*. The crisis of our parishes today is evident, among many other signs, also in the fact that there is scarcely anything like sisterly or brotherly correction in the biblical sense, even though Paul speaks of it so often (cf., e.g., Rom 15:14; Gal 6:1; 1 Thess 5:14).

Especially characteristic of the Pauline mission are the many house churches that are referred to both in Acts (18:7; 20:8, 20) and in the Pauline letters (Rom 16:5; 1 Cor 16:19; Col 4:15; Phlm 2). The communities met in the houses of wealthy members (cf. Acts 12:12), and the latter made not only their houses but often their very lives

[2] *Dia tēs agapēs douleuete allēlois.* NRSVue, NRSV literal translation: "become slaves." The NABRE softens this to "serve one another."—Tr.

available for the building up of communities. We get a good glimpse of such Christian togetherness in the house of the Jewish couple Prisca and Aquila, where many Christians gathered—in Corinth, later in Ephesus, and finally in Rome. In particular it was the house churches in which Christians grew together, in the celebration of the Lord's Supper, to form the "Body of Christ."[3]

Paul grounds the "togetherness" in the community with his statement that this is the "body of Christ" (1 Cor 12:27) or by speaking of it as "one body in Christ" (Rom 12:5). Ultimately this ecclesiological metaphor is based in the tradition of the Lord's Supper (1 Cor 10:16-17). In it, Christ's surrender of his life and the power of his resurrection join Christians together and enable Christian sisterly and brotherly love, *agapē*.

Above all, this *agapē* is the power given by the Holy Spirit that enables and characterizes togetherness in the community. To that extent it is not simply to be identified with the utopia of universal love for humanity, as too often happens, alas. For Paul the noun *agapē* (and the verb *agapaō*) refer to community life, just as in the Johannine letters (see especially Rom 13:8; Gal 5:13; 1 Thess 4:9). In speaking of a relationship *to* non-Christians or *their* actions Paul prefers to speak of "doing good" (Rom 2:10; Gal 6:10; 1 Thess 5:15).

This intense awareness that, as based in Christ, the community is a single body bound together in sibling love corresponds to the contrast-function of a Christian community over against pagan society (Rom 12:2; Phil 2:14-15). Paul and his students worked out that contrast-function in a number of ways, above all by using the pattern of "formerly . . . but now" (Rom 6:19; 2 Cor 5:17; Eph 5:8; Titus 3:3-7), then by contrasting pagan vices with the "fruits of the Spirit" (Gal 5:19-26), or with the use of the concept of "sanctification" (Rom 6:19; 1 Cor 6:11; 1 Thess 4:2-8). Anyone in Germany (and many other places) today who refers to that former contrast-function of Christian communities will find no friends in the church. Instead of "contrast," it is now preferable to speak of the necessary "compatibility" of church and society or even to

[3] Thus Peter Stuhlmacher, excursus "Urchristliche Hausgemeinden," in his *Der Brief an Philemon*, EKK 18 (Düsseldorf: Benziger; Neukirchen-Vluyn: Neukirchener Verlag, 2nd ed. 1981), 70–75, at 74.

emphasize that the church's *ethos* must be one of "easy access" or of having a "low threshold."

That last statement gives a hint of the whole problematic of subsequent times when the church of martyrs and confessors was gradually transformed into an "imperial church." The tiny communities that, in terms of their whole situation and history, stood in contrast to pagan society developed between the fourth and sixth centuries into units of governance to which everyone in the empire must belong. Being Christian was no longer a matter of free decision; it was a social requirement, and the "*parochia*," that is, the parish, all too often was no longer the *locus* of a vital experience of Christianity.

Naturally, I cannot describe here the course of this step-by-step transformation of the formerly freely chosen church into a comprehensive imperial church. I can only point to what almost necessarily had to happen within the church as a result of that development: the repeated rise of new communities that sought what had characterized the early church despite all its failures, guilt, and divisions: that there is such a thing as a free decision in favor of a Christian existence, discipleship, living on the basis of the Gospel, the joining of lives, the *vita apostolica*.

Beginning in the fourth century (and even earlier in Egypt, which so quickly became Christian) many Christians turned to a radical life of asceticism and internalization of Sacred Scripture. This was most obvious (especially in Egypt) in the "withdrawal into the desert." Whole colonies of hermits or anchorites were established. Certainly there were many reasons for this "exodus"—for example, the pressure of taxation or compulsory military recruitment. More important was a motivation stemming from ancient philosophy: that true insight and wisdom were only to be acquired through a life of strict asceticism. But for many Christians the decisive reason for the exodus was different: above all the longing, already named, to live the whole Gospel to the full. It was precisely at the time when church communities were losing their earlier closeness to the Gospel that the exodus of the anchorites and monks began. That correspondence in time cannot have been an accident.

In the beginning this exodus was in fact a flight from the world into individual solitude, but that would change very quickly. Quite soon the withdrawal of early Christian ascetics to the desert took on a specifically "Christian" form through the men and women who created a community movement from the ascetic withdrawal. First and foremost among them was the Egyptian Pachomius, who is the progenitor of cenobitic monasticism. In about 320/325 he founded the monastery of Tabennisi in Upper Egypt. By the end of his life Pachomius had founded nine cloisters for men and, with the aid of his sister, two for women. In all they housed more than ten thousand monks and nuns.

Thus the isolated lives of many hermits yielded to table fellowship, common prayer, organized work in common: the with-one-another and for-one-another of a "new family" in the gospel sense (Mark 3:34-35). In this way something of what had existed in Christian communities from the beginning was carried forward and given a new form in the midst of a society that was sinking into a Christianity of habit.

This community movement that began in the fourth century has not ceased to this day. More and more new orders and institutes of common life, new spiritual communities and movements, have established themselves, sustained by the longing for a radical life according to the Gospel and moved by longing for a solid community in faith. The relevant texts were Jesus' instructions for disciples (esp. Matt 19:16-30), the summaries in Acts (esp. Acts 2:43-47), and Paul's exhortations to his communities (esp. Rom 12:1-21).

It is impossible to give even an overview of the incredible multitude and variety of those church-community institutions. Let me just list, from the perspective of the Catholic churches, the various *forms* of such conjoinings apart from the usual parishes: there are societies of monks following the Rule of St. Benedict. Since the mid-eleventh century there have been the so-called "Canons Regular," following the Rule of Augustine—for example, the Augustinian canons and the Premonstratensians. In the thirteenth century arose the preaching orders of Dominicans and Franciscans, with a completely new structure from that in the Rule of St. Benedict. The sixteenth century saw the beginning of the Jesuit order, again with a new and revolutionary form in which mission, availability for service, and mobility play a central role; also there arose so-called "Communities of Apostolic Life" such as the Oratorians.

Orders of women were founded in parallel to nearly all those for men, not only devoted to contemplation but later also for instruction in schools, care of the sick, and the apostolate. Especially in the nineteenth century there arose seemingly innumerable congregations of women: that is, communities whose members took only "simple vows" and were especially active in the social sphere. Likewise characteristic of the nineteenth century was the rise of many missionary societies such as the White Fathers or the Spiritans.

In the year 1933 René Voillaume founded the Little Brothers of Jesus, based on the life of Charles de Foucauld; they were quickly followed by the Little Sisters of Jesus. This was a new form of order, for the most part outwardly directed, whose members simply wanted to live among the poor and share their lives. Comparable to them, to a degree, is the multitude of so-called "secular institutes" from the twentieth century. Since the middle of that century a number of new spiritual communities have arisen: these include *Comunione e liberazione*, the "Neo-catechumenate," the *Focolare* movement, the community of *Sant' Egidio*, the "Immanuel" community, and "Cursillo," to mention only a few.

Still, with all that the list of different types of common life is far from being exhausted, because there are yet other and very different forms of life shaped by the Gospel in the history of the church. In the first centuries, for example, there were so-called family- or house-monasteries in which a single family—usually well-to-do—gathered friends around itself and tried to live discipleship of Jesus together with them. In the Middle Ages and in the Baroque period the so-called "brotherhoods" played an outstanding role. We may also mention the "Third Orders" (tertiaries)—societies of Roman Catholic laypersons, most of them married, that formed around one or another of the classic orders. Or we may think of the Beguines and Begardes (since the twelfth century), and the Brothers and Sisters of the Common Life (since the fourteenth century). Or there were the Christian villages in the Jesuit Reductions in South America (seventeenth/eighteenth centuries). Or again there were Christian villages in East Africa, founded by the Spiritans in the nineteenth century, made up of enslaved persons whose freedom had been purchased. All of these led, from morning to night, a life deliberately Christian in form, even similar to that of the Orders—but as married persons. A great many more could be named as well.

In particular I should now list corresponding spiritual communities and movements within the churches of the Reformation and characterize them according to type—from the Herrnhuter Brothers through Dietrich Bonhoeffer's Bruderhaus, to the Bruderhof and on to the Brothers of Jesus and many other recent community foundations beyond the official parish or community. But that would far exceed the limits of this overview. It is more important to draw a conclusion from what has been said thus far. Let me begin with the early communities of monks and nuns. The Rule of Saint Augustine says at the very beginning:

> The main purpose for you having come together is to live harmoniously in your house, intent upon God in oneness of mind and heart. (*Rule* I.2)

The reference to Acts 4:32 is clear. The monastic community is to be a "new family" in the sense of the gospels and Acts. Hans Urs von Balthasar once observed that this longing for the church at its origins stands at the beginning of all the great monastic rules.

But if there were to be a "*new* family" it would necessarily involve something of a new society, a new culture, and a transformed world. In fact, many monasteries that began as new foundations in inhospitable places very quickly became successful centers of enterprise. They shaped their environment not only in faith but also in civilization and culture. Hence it is again clear that faith must become incarnate. It cannot be unworldly. By its very nature it is directed toward penetrating all the circumstances of believers' lives and giving them a new and redeemed shape. Of itself, faith presses toward changing social relationships and shaping the material of the world. It is no longer clear to many Europeans (and others) today how much the world in which they live has been civilized and humanized by Christian faith.

In any case the Western monasteries carried on the exodus character of the people of God. Above all in times when almost no one had the freedom *not to be a Christian*, they symbolized the freedom to follow Jesus. At the same time they maintained something of the earlier community church with their practice of common faith and living.

Certainly there were some dangerous developments in Western monasticism. Regrettably, the freedom I have referred to was restricted in the early Middle Ages by the institution of *oblatio*, whereby children were dedicated to monastic life by their parents. Any attempt on their part to leave the monastery at a later time brought with it excommunication (Fourth Council of Toledo). It was the monastery at Cluny that first sought to minimize the numbers of oblates in its own cloisters, and the Cistercians were the first who, in principle, accepted no oblates. Still, the practice continued in many monasteries and brought immense harm to the monastic communities. Another abuse was the medieval proprietary church system, which led to many monasteries falling into the hands of noble landlords who protected the cloisters while simultaneously treating them as family property and exploiting them as such. Nevertheless, despite all the abuses, the monasteries were an overflowing blessing for the church. The same is true of the later communities in which faith in the Gospel took on shape and spirit.

It must also be said that the monasteries in particular, and their exceptional role in the history of the West (and equally so in the East), represented a loss, too: while they regarded themselves as monastic "families" they always consisted only of men or only of women. At least in the Catholic Church—with a few important exceptions over many centuries—there was no such thing for married persons as discipleship in a biblically-shaped way of life.

It is true that countless mothers and fathers lived exodus and discipleship, usually in silence and in hidden ways—namely, in the form of a love of neighbor that not so rarely led to the sacrifice of their lives. Still, the aid of a lively Christian community was often denied them. In particular, for a long time they had no opportunity to put their common life to use in the proclamation of the Gospel and service to the community.

The situation was different with the churches of the Reformation. Let me again mention here, as an especially prominent example, the worldwide communities of the Herrnhuter (Moravians). Many other examples could be given, especially communitarian structures in the so-called "free churches." In Germany in recent decades it is especially in the Lutheran and Protestant communities that an extraordinary number of house churches have emerged, in which people read the Scriptures together, pray, and invite people who are strangers to the church to enter into dialogue.

Beginning in the twentieth century, and especially since Vatican II, there have been increasing numbers of spiritual communities and movements in which not only single people but families share their lives. I have already listed some. In this regard we must speak of a new awakening both in the Roman Catholic Church and in the churches of the Reformation.

The reason for this awakening, among many other things, is a renewed view of the Bible, which now also has a scholarly foundation. It is no accident that at the beginning of these reflections I spoke of the will of God to have a "people" in the world—indeed, a people that continually lives the Exodus and that forms a unity in faith and life. Another reason, however, for the growth of new spiritual communities is that the society in which we live is more and more sharply segmented; many people seek a lifestyle for themselves as individuals, with free associations that often remain non-binding. Obviously this unwillingness to maintain ties has a massive effect on parish life. Still, more and more Christians are sensing that Christian "community," of its very nature, is more than attendance at Sunday worship and vowed life in orders and religious communities.

Still, the communitarian association of Christian families also brings with it problems that did not exist in the same way in the classic orders and that were probably among the reasons why the Catholic Church suppressed communitarian groups of families or at least regarded them with extreme skepticism: I am thinking here especially of the upbringing of children and, together with it, protection of the necessary intimacy of the family. Children need their natural families and teens need the freedom (age-appropriate, of course) to make decisions about their own lives.

It is also the case that adults must choose a communitarian life *in complete freedom*. But with their decision they accept obligations that youth cannot yet adopt in that form, and indeed they should not do so. This matter of free—and enduringly free—acceptance is the crucial question for all spiritual communities, and a great deal depends on it.

For that very reason it makes sense at this point to look back again at the strategies Jesus adopted for his eschatological gathering of Israel. He demonstrates an unusual and surprising openness and acceptance:

a) Here we find the circle of the Twelve and that of the disciples, with the corresponding *ethos* of discipleship. And as we have seen: the group of disciples was at the center of Jesus' initiative in incarnating the reign of God.

b) There are also people resident in different places who do not travel with Jesus through Israel but whose most important duty is to receive the disciples into their houses at night, feed them, and support them.

c) Beyond these there are friends, sympathizers, and helpers of the Jesus movement, people Jesus does not take into the circle of disciples but instead sends home to tell about what he is doing (e.g., Mark 5:18-20).

d) And on the margins of the Jesus movement there are even those who take advantage of Jesus' cause, not joining him but profiting from his movement—for example, the man who drives out demons in Jesus' name (Mark 9:38-39). The disciples want to make him stop, but Jesus' humorous and pragmatic judgment on him is: "At least he can't say anything bad about me."

This incredible openness on the part of Jesus and the strategy of concentric circles would also be important for all new church communities. There has to be discipleship in them, but there must also be many others who surround that center and are stimulated by it to live their Christian life based on their baptismal promises, without imitating the commitment involved in discipleship.

At the outset I spoke at some length in biblical terms about the nature of the people of God and community. That was necessary. "Community" as Luke and Paul envisioned it is the proper internal structure of the people of God, adopted from Israel. And in every community (or parish)—depending on the concrete callings of individuals—there should also be discipleship, a new exodus from negative patterns in the society, and also people who offer their whole lives for the building up of the community.

Because, from the fourth century onward, that no longer existed in many places and Christianity all too often lost its salt, the various monasteries, and later the spiritual communities, became "representatives" of the Exodus and of New Testament-oriented communities. This elementary relationship to church as community is also visible in the fact that in the early days of monasticism no special vows were taken. The monks and sisters regarded their baptism as their vow. When, later, profession was introduced into the Orders, it was seen as a realization and actualization of baptism.

For that very reason monasteries and spiritual communities have something preliminary about them: the goal must be parishes that continually relate themselves to the Bible and allow themselves to be renewed by it. For that very reason cloisters and spiritual communities have a sign-character. They are not islands, nor are they refuges for the fulfillment of Christian life. They exist for the sake of the church—and thus for the plan God has for the world.

It may be that, after this forced march through biblical theology and church history, my readers can better understand why I left Tübingen, together with my parents, and joined the *Integrierte Gemeinde*. It was because in it I found the effort to realize everything—really everything—that I have just so summarily described.

I found regular "assembly" (let us remember that "church" in Greek means nothing other than "assembly"). Not only Sunday morning Mass but also the afternoons or evenings on the day before were assemblies that joined everyone together and in which all knew each other, rejoicing or sorrowing together.

I found the "from feast to feast" that was and is so characteristic of Israel. What feasts we celebrated! Anchored in the salvation history of the people of God—and at the same time with new songs, much telling of stories, dancing, and common meals. It was in Munich and in the affiliated communities in Walchensee, Wangen, Hagen, Vienna, Rome, and Tanzania that I really experienced for the first time what a "feast" can be.

I found what mutual solidarity meant, already in the book of Leviticus (there as "love of neighbor") and then for Jesus: generous help was given to my parents to make them comfortable in Munich; when they grew ill they received care from nurses and doctors in the community. I myself was welcomed, simply as a matter of course, by members or friends of the community whenever I traveled, for example to give a lecture—and I could never begin to describe all the technical and personal help that was given me in the past four decades by so many brothers and sisters.

In addition: *I could again and again experience what the Bible calls the "gathering of God's people."* Christians from Austria, Italy, Switzerland, and the United States came to us because they were seeking a community based on the Bible. Often they remained with us. Sometimes whole groups came with everything they had: for example, at Easter 1990 we received a group of young people from Hungary. As early as 1977 a bishop from Tanzania had come to us in the course of a trip through Europe to meet with new Christian communities. He wanted to establish such groups in his diocese. He remained for some time, inspected everything closely, returned to his diocese, and then sent us a large number of young Africans to learn a trade and receive a good education from us that they could use to help establish communities in Tanzania. I participated for a long time in teaching them German so that they could absorb the instructions for their trade or business.

Still more: *In Acts there are narratives about how new communities or missionary advances came about, often quite unexpectedly and without planning. I was able to experience precisely the same thing happening with us.* The visit from the Tanzanian bishop, Christopher Mwoleka, led us in 1987 to send some of our own members to Tanzania. There, in Melela Bustani, we established a large farm (with a carpentry and mechanics' workshop nearby). Melela was intended to be the basis for a community and at the same time to offer young Africans the opportunity to receive a thorough education in agronomy. We knew that Africa needs experienced craftspeople and farmers. In 1994 we were able to adopt a parish in Mikese (Tanzania) and then, gradually, to build a new church, a school, and a boarding school for girls within the bounds of the parish. The boarding school was important primarily because many girls who lived far away in the bush and widely separated from one another would otherwise have had no chance of finishing school and learning a trade or profession.

Finally, I could also experience how priestly callings emerged within the community itself. In the beginning a number of priests came to us after being released by their bishops or religious orders. (Sometimes they came out of great personal need.) But then priests emerged in the community itself. We were even able to establish an association of priests and, in cooperation with a number of bishops, to assume leadership of parishes—in Hergensweiler, Walchensee, Vienna-Neuhaus, and then in Africa. The same process is familiar from the experience of other new spiritual movements. That the number of priests in Germany, and in Europe as a whole, is shrinking drastically thus need not point to an inevitable fate.

I should mention many other things that revealed to me the points of contact between our communities and the Old and New Testaments. That was what gave me my deepest joy and what I had named in my farewell lecture in Tübingen: vital discipleship, living from the Gospel, mutual joining of lives, table companionship, co-responsibility for the faith of others. What was crucial in all of it was that we found a new and more profound relationship to the Old Testament and thus also to Judaism, to Jesus' proclamation of the reign of God, and to the church.

My parents died a long time ago: my father at age ninety, my mother at ninety-four—both of them cared for lovingly in the Gemeinde. I myself live now with a couple from the community in a large rented house, write books on biblical subjects, and rejoice when I again and again hear good news from so many brothers and sisters who have followed the same path as I.

That brings me to the end of this chapter. The *Integrierte Gemeinde* in Germany was stripped by the bishops of its recognition as an "apostolic community." The revocation proper took place in Munich. Against the background of what I have written, my dear readers, you may understand why I cannot describe the decades-long prehistory and then the course of the revocation. Historians may be in a position to do so elsewhere.

12

Defending God

If this book were nothing but an autobiography I should speak now of *the* part of my life we call the "end": that is, the time when hearing fades, walking becomes a shaky business, visits to the doctor increase, the medicine chest is overflowing—and more and more friends and acquaintances are no longer here.

But since this book is not just autobiographical, but more about theological questions—above all the question of questions, *whether there is a God*—I will speak now not about the beautiful things I experience more intensively with age (nor about all the frustrations no one can avoid). Instead I want to address a question that has arisen for me more and more in recent years—*namely, that of the immeasurable misery of the world in which we live, and whether the well-nigh endless series of wars and catastrophes can be reconciled with faith in God*. So now it is about the problem of theodicy, the justification of God.

It is not as if this question did not exist for me earlier in my life. It stirred itself, at least: I lost two beloved sisters. My elder sister Marianne was torn to bits by an American bomber in 1944 in the railroad station of a small city in the Rhön mountains, together with more than sixty other schoolchildren. I have already mentioned that. Later, my younger sister Margarete, at the age of nine, was run over by a streetcar. My mother was called to the scene, and before her eyes a crane lifted the streetcar so that the bloody corpse of my little sister could be pulled out of the wheel rods of the tram. I was not there, but I was told that my mother knelt on the asphalt and prayed.

I myself was too young and too ignorant to begin to understand how parents felt in such situations. I had previously experienced some of the wartime bombing without really grasping what was going on. In the late fall of 1944 (when we were bombed out of our home and all had to flee to relatives in the Rhön mountains) I was sometimes in the field with the farmers, gathering the potatoes that had been plowed to the surface, when low-flying fighter planes appeared and shot at us. The farmers would then dive under the wagons laden with heavy sacks of potatoes. I myself had always looked ahead of time for a deep hole close to the field, and that was where I crouched as soon as the bombers appeared in the distance, thinking "You'll never get me!" Treating a horrible war incited by Hitler as a kind of "war game"—that is how naïve children that age can be. In those days we also collected fragments of grenades and traded them like stamps. Whoever had the biggest fragment was the object of friends' admiration.

Today I am experiencing war again—not yet directly where I live, but fairly near and brought still closer by modern media. Now it is entirely different for me. I am seized by profound rage when I am present, through words and images, as an autocrat who rules a huge empire attacks Ukraine, and when I see how he deliberately assaults the civilian population with drones and rockets to demoralize them.

Today I cannot cope when I am present on October 7, 2023, through words and images, at the attack by Hamas on unsuspecting people, the rape of women, the dismembering of children, the murder of 1,200 Israeli and foreign civilians, the abduction of 240 hostages into mile-long subterranean passages, while they continually spread the lie that the fault lies entirely with the criminal Jews—and I see that even in the West a shocking number of people, many of them highly intelligent, readily believe Hamas.[1]

And today I no longer know what to think when, in the United States, a candidate for president is seeking to destroy American democracy and his followers gather in crowds to cheer him—and he really has a chance of winning the next presidential election—to

[1] This was written before the extent of Israeli violence against the people of Gaza emerged.—Tr.

say nothing of all the despots, violent autocrats, and invaders in the rest of the world who drive their peoples into dire poverty that results in greater and greater streams of migrants.

How can God permit such a thing? Despite the countless petitions throughout the world for peace and justice? That troubles me more and more. It crushes me. But what increasingly presses on me—in addition to the immeasurable suffering that repeatedly falls on so many—is the crisis of so many believers who cannot deal with it all. For many, very many believing Christians it has become a question about God.

Therefore this book must address the question, but the search for an answer demands a long approach. I want to begin "at the bottom," namely, with biology and evolution, and thus make my way slowly to the problem itself.

⚜

So we should not start with the political criminals! All that is needed at the beginning is to look at purely biological suffering: proliferating cancer cells, multiple sclerosis, creeping dementia, so many illnesses for which there is still no cure, new diseases that did not exist before—Ebola, for example. People in West Africa who become infected with the Ebola virus must expect a mortality rate of fifty percent. And then at the end, for all of us, no matter what the cause, there is death and decay.

How could God create such a world? Doesn't it all testify against a good and loving God? How can God stand behind a creation in which disgusting, repulsive, and constant death happens? Reinhold Schneider, in his *Winter in Wien*, could find no answer to self-devouring Nature. After a visit to the Vienna Museum of Natural History he wrote about the Japanese crabs he had seen there, who seemed to him as if they had emerged from the *Inferno*. Then he describes how a frog, "standing erect like a human being, was sucked dry by a leech that had wrapped itself around it." He speaks in the same context of the "absurd architecture" of the dinosaurs, calling them "cathedrals of futility," the "will to live that cannot live." Then comes the statement:

> What is so scary is that human forms are at play in the monsters: the dinosaur's knee recalls the human knee, and the characteristic number of five fingers and toes is latent even in the flippers of the sea elephant. The loveliest bird snatches the most beautiful butterfly in flight, plucks off its wings and lets them float away while devouring the tender body that, during its brief existence, was satisfied with just a little nectar and, unprotected, bestowed on the world the play of color in its wings, a blaze from the hands of the Father. Likewise, so it seems, a beetle with a green-gold shimmer was created to destroy the rose. I saw one at work in Muzot.[2] Unclean contradiction, it spared not one. And the Father's face? It is altogether unfathomable.[3]

That, of course, is an enormous issue that has disturbed people for centuries: Nature's pattern of devouring and being devoured. What can I say about the subject in such a short chapter? I might begin with this:

We dare not charge God with the things we find biologically repugnant. That birds eat butterflies and beetles devour roses is simply part of our world, which includes becoming and decay, birth and death, and even eating and being eaten. *The constant battle to which belong becoming and passing away is—from a biological point of view—simply part of life.*

For example: in every second of our lives there is an unceasing warfare going on in the microworld of the body, which is steadily attacked by agents of disease that are not part of us: bacteria, viruses, fungi, and parasites that seek to spread through our bodies and assault our healthy cells. Our immune system has to deal with this constant invasion by microorganisms. So it calls its police forces, such as T-cells, into battle. A merciless war goes on in our systems between the sources of disease and the corresponding molecular police. There is mutual killing and eating. Without this ongoing battle within us, our lives would end very quickly. Then,

[2] The reference is to the last home of Rainer Maria Rilke, the Château de Muzot in the Swiss canton of Valais.

[3] Reinhold Schneider, *Winter in Wien. Aus meinen Notizbüchern 1957/58* (Freiburg: Herder, 6th ed. 1961), 129–31. Translation LMM.

for example, we would all quite rapidly succumb to cancer because our bodies could not deal with rogue cells.

Unending combat goes on even in our mouths. It is a vast mistake to suppose that after one has brushed one's teeth the mouth is germ-free. More than two hundred kinds of microbes constantly populate the mucus-clad space between our lips and our gums. (Of course, only a minority are harmful. The larger number of bacteria in our mouths serve as a kind of sanitary police promoting the health of our gums and teeth.) So here, too: unbounded zeal for devouring, reckless battle, and uninterrupted killing on the microbiological level. If that never-ending war did not take place our teeth would very soon fall out.

All that is simply part of evolution, of life. That we are alive at all, that we can breathe, that we are surrounded by the right atmosphere, that here on our blue planet are air and life-sustaining water—all that is an unbelievable balancing act. We should, therefore, not be shocked or frightened by this constant peril, this existence in the midst of death. It is one of the miracles of life. We could even propose a formula:

Without death, no new life.

Without ever-new life, no sequence of generations.

Without a sequence of generations, no evolution.

Without evolution, no history.

Without history, no freedom.

And without freedom, no love.

But I need to explain that more precisely. The first line is clear: *without death, no new life*. If there were no death on the earth the biotopes would literally explode; there would be no more space for life; the room for every living thing would be reduced more and more; there would be no more air to support life; not-dying would, indeed, mean death for all living things. In short: every generation has to make room for the next one. That is as true for people as for microbes; it applies to every living thing.

The second and third lines are equally clear: *without constantly new life there could be no sequence of generations, and without that sequence there could be no evolution.* The evolution of living things is only possible because genes mutate. Without that, the genome would always stay the same. The enormous variety of living things could never have come to be. Organs such as eyes and ears would not have developed. There would be no mammals. Human beings, with their enormous ability to adapt, their intelligence, their self-extension toward ever-new goals, their longings and their hopes, would never have come to be.

The third statement, too, almost speaks for itself: *without evolution there could be no history.* If we try to imagine that human development had stopped with *Homo erectus* it becomes obvious that these ancestors of *Homo sapiens* would have had no sense of history. Herodotus and Thucydides would never have been possible. This is because, for humans, evolution is always also cultural. In fact, the cultural evolution that builds on biological evolution and that of civilizations steadily becomes richer and more consequential for humans.

The line one might most easily doubt is the fourth: *without history, no freedom.* But I beg my readers at this point to consider: what is the basis on which genuinely free decisions, which are not an everyday thing, have come about? It was always because others have made our freedom possible. All the spaces for freedom that open to us humans exist only because others have preceded us in freedom. The result is a long chain of free decisions and, throughout history, an increasing number of experiences of freedom that are a precondition for our own. The statement "without history, no freedom" is, in my opinion, fundamental, because freedom does not fall from heaven. It came out of the animal kingdom in an infinitely slow process, and it still has to be fought for and mediated to us—by the valor and initiative of many others. Freedom, just like unfreedom, comes to us from history.

Then the sixth line: *without freedom, no love*—do I have to prove that? Those who have grasped that genuine love extends beyond *eros* and sexuality know that freedom is essential to love. Without free attachment, free sympathy, love remains unfulfilled. That is true not only of love that involves sexuality but of every kind of human affection and solidarity. Freedom is an incredible existential. It is only in freedom that the human becomes truly such. It is only when love is altogether free and unearned that its brilliance and beauty emerge.

Now we can move backwards: genuine love presupposes freedom; freedom, history; history, evolution; evolution, the sequence of generations—and that sequence presupposes death. Thus dying is a necessary part of our world. It cannot immediately be seen in itself as something negative.

Now, however, another crucial element emerges. We do not simply live in a world that corresponds to God's creative will. We inhabit a world that has already been shaped by a long history of sin and guilt. Human history is saturated with a sequence of refusals to approach God. I could say the same thing in another way: human history is filled with a sequence of refusals to apply one's own reason and to be in solidarity with other people. However, the refusal to do what could be done, to realize the truth and freedom that could exist in the world, creates a potential for guilt and thus a narrowing of perspective. Legacies of human guilt build up and darken our field of vision. We are all surrounded by a history that is in no way innocent any longer. I already wrote at length in Chapter 7 about this process, to which the church has given the easily misunderstood name "original [or: inherited] sin." Let me add this: in reality the world should mirror the glory of God, but it does not, or at least not fully. The potentialities for guilt throughout history dim and veil our eyes.

As a result of such potential for evil, because of such obscurings of our sight, we are often utterly unable to recognize God's creation in its meaningfulness and beauty. Our sight is darkened. Too often we cannot even understand what creation truly is. The so-called "evils" such as natural catastrophes, sickness, and death are part of the world with its finitude and historicity. But because of the history of human sin and its ancient burdens, the quality of these "evils" has changed. We see them through dark glasses, through a veil. We see them dimmed. We can no longer understand them directly, within the horizon of a dimension of meaning given by God.

Thus, for example, we see death not as a transition to God but as a terrifying and tragic termination of our lives. Or we experience nature not as God's manifold and colorful creation but as a profound and even dangerous enemy of the human. It is not nature itself that is evil or repulsive or disgusting—but that is often how it appears to us.

For example, the opinion whether an animal is hideous or beautiful is altogether subjective. I knew a professor of biology who specialized in research on spiders. He found that they are not only useful but truly elegant creatures. His wife, on the other hand, always had a fit if she saw a spider in the house. Please do not say that such disgust is only related to the struggle for cleanliness. It is more deep-seated. It is often rooted in defensive reactions from our animal past that warn us of danger. Hence, for example, our aversion to anything slimy and everything that seems alien. To that extent such reactions are, in fact, justified, but they also prevent us from seeing creation objectively—we may simply say: from perceiving it in its purposefulness, variety, and beauty.

Certainly the atavistic fear of spiders and mice has its amusing side. But when the same reflex appears as soon as we encounter people whose skin is a different color or whose face is a different shape, who speak and behave differently—who, in short, are strangers to us—it immediately becomes clear what I mean by "veiling of our sight." We then, all too often, immediately regard people who are different from us as intruders, opponents, and enemies. Then it is usually impossible for us to recognize them as *human beings* placed at our side so that we can work with them and provide mutual aid. Instead we see them as competitors and are afraid of them—and all too often they are shunned, excluded, hated, and persecuted.

That brings me, finally, to the point that is central to the question of suffering in the world. Yes, the world contains dreadful and horrifying things. But all too often we do not set any obstacles to the evils of the world, even though they could be thwarted—and often we ourselves produce such evils. There is a great deal of human suffering that simply need not happen.

Many natural catastrophes would not prove fatal to anyone if people worked together in solidarity. In regions where earthquakes are common, earthquake-proof houses could be built. There could be early warning ahead of tsunamis; the same is true of sudden floods and tornadoes. Likewise, the persistent famines in certain parts of the world need not happen. They are not caused only by changes in the climate; they often have political backgrounds.

Or think of the floods of refugees who are driven from their homes or abandon them because they can no longer exist there. The steadily increasing migration now breaking over Europe did not have to happen. It is people—the powerful, criminals, warmongers—who have caused and continue to cause a superfluity of human misery.

Does that make everything clear, and can I close this chapter? No! Nothing is clear. It all had to be said, but the question of "God and the world's suffering" has much more profound dimensions.

For example, there is Auschwitz. There is the Shoah. In the context of the question about suffering in the world, Auschwitz maintains an awkward resistance to every attempt at a theological explanation. The murder of six million Jews remains an incomprehensible event, almost a new kind of happening in the face of which today's theology would prefer to keep silent.

Auschwitz and all the other death camps ignite, anew and with ultimate radicality, the question of suffering in the world: how can God permit the endless misery in history, above all what has been imposed on God's own people? Hasn't Auschwitz put an end to the God-question, once and for all? Shouldn't the fate of defenseless children, women, and old people who were driven naked into the gas ovens have lacerated God's heart? If there is a God, that is.

I can say all that follows here only with the prior reservation that in the face of such events our first reaction should be silence. In reality I should have spoken of that silence at the beginning of this chapter. But we cannot fall silent on command. My chapter had to have a beginning, and it must continue here. What I mean by saying "fall silent" must continue as an undercurrent. It should wordlessly accompany everything that is said about suffering in the world, and above all it should saturate and sustain all argument with rational grounding.

Together with such silence, the biblical prayer-genre of lament should accompany all theological rhetoric about God and suffering. It breaks forth, for example, in the first half of Psalm 22:

> My God, O my God, why have you forsaken me?
> Why are you so far from helping me, from the words of my groaning?
> O my God, I cry by day, but you do not answer;
> and by night but find no rest.
> . . .
> For dogs are all around me;
> a company of evildoers encircles me;
> they bound my hands and feet.
> I can count all my bones.
> They stare and gloat over me;
> they divide my clothes among themselves,
> and for my clothing they cast lots. (Ps 22:2-3, 17-19)

Who is the "I" who speaks here? As a modern person one naturally thinks of an individual, a single person in severe distress. That is not wrong, but it does not touch the true depth-dimension of the psalm because the "I" of the Psalms and Lamentations in the Old Testament is almost always the "we" of Israel. All Israel is here lamenting before God, crying out over the horrors of its history, the misery the nations bring upon it. Or else it groans over the suffering that some among the people of God impose on others. Psalm 22 is, to begin with, pure lament, and that lament demands extended space before the psalm turns to God in full trust and hope.

In the same way there must also be space for lament when we people of the present look at the world's suffering. We should not even begin to think about the question of God and suffering before we have made a place for lament. That is true even for the modern pagans who are so appalled that the world is a slaughterhouse—for without this shocked and sorrowful lament all reflection on suffering will reduce itself to mere reasoning. Insofar as lament constantly remembers, it will sustain itself in what has happened and continually participate in it anew. Still, Psalm 22 does not stop with lament. It transforms itself into a plea:

> But you, O Lord, do not be far away;
> my strength, come quickly to help me.
> Deliver my life from the sword,
> my sole possession from the grip of the dog.

> Save me from the vengeance of the lion,
> from the horns of wild bulls! (Ps 22:20-22; author's translation)

Then, at the end of the Psalm, God has intervened and rescued the one who cried for help, who now celebrates a festal meal with relatives and friends during which the story of this rescue is told.

But how did God save in Israel at that time? And how does God save today? How were those deported to Babylon and the hungry people who remained in the Land snatched from their misery? And how did God help the Jews as they were driven together, jammed into boxcars, borne eastward, separated into groups, and then sent to perish from lethal toil or deadly gas? Was it by reaching down from above? By performing a miracle? By an earthquake that terrified the SS and moved them to convert? Through a plague that eliminated all the Nazis? By causing Hitler, Himmler, Eichmann, and their consorts to drop dead? There has been nothing of the sort in history thus far.

In fact, Hitler was devilishly lucky. He escaped a number of attempts on his life. If there was ever a case in which evil was driven away, we immediately think of contrary instances: goodness has also been and is still being snatched away. So now and in the future we cannot count on any saving magic of that kind. No fire fell from heaven on Auschwitz to immolate the SS troops. But in that case, how does God act? After all, the whole Bible takes it for granted that God helps, saves, intervenes.

The answer can only be that God acts through people—women and men who believe in God, are seized with God's Spirit, and have no further fear of dictators because they live out of the words of Scripture: "We must obey God rather than human beings" (Acts 5:29).

God has truly acted in this way. There were more than a few people who hid Jews at the risk of their own lives, or who helped them escape, or who preached from the pulpit about the Fifth Commandment in such a way that everyone got the message. Bernhard Lichtenberg, provost of the cathedral in Berlin, protested to the National Socialist authorities, repeatedly petitioning them against what was happening in the concentration camps. He prayed publicly for the Jews and all the persecuted; for that he was arrested, tortured, and died while being transported to Dachau. Many priests whose preaching had made them unpopular with the Gestapo suffered in Dachau itself.

Sadly, there were too few who thus allowed God to act. Certainly God works through people, but above all through the people God has created as God's own. The meaning of the people of God is solely that God needs a people in the world who are a blessing for others, who overcome violence with nonviolence, and who are on the side of the poor. It is through this people, above all, that God wants to save; this people is God's instrument for the world.

But that means that Christians in Germany as a whole should not have dared to permit their Jewish sisters and brothers to be excluded: branded with a Star of David, socially despised, and exposed to more and more oppression. At the latest when the windows of Jewish businesses were smashed by the SA and synagogues were set alight—then, at the very latest, Christian communities in Germany should have taken to the streets and declared themselves in solidarity with the Jews.

Hitler would have been rendered powerless.

It did not happen. A centuries-long history of Christian anti-Judaism and a false respect for state authority blinded the eyes and darkened the minds of those who should have acted. So, did God fail to act? No, it was the majority of Christians in Germany who did not act. Was God silent? No, Christians were. Did God look away? No, we ourselves did.

To many pious people it may still seem peculiar to say such things: extreme, one-sided, not very churchly, deviating too much from the usual religious jargon. But this kind of irritating talk can determine whether we will finally reject our false God-images and the evil they create in the world.

God is not a stopgap or someone who occasionally intervenes in the world's business—when it suits, or when it comes to mind. If that were the case, then God decided not to meddle with Auschwitz; it didn't please God to do so. Such words are blasphemy. God is always acting, continually sending the divine Spirit so that Christianity may wake up and accept its responsibility.

God wants to act in the world through believers. Everything depends on whether they listen to God or prefer to close their ears and look away.

This makes it clear what an enormous responsibility, terrifying independence, and breathtaking freedom God affords to humanity. Ultimately the whole question we are dealing with here culminates in the awesome reality of human freedom and responsibility.

Still, all that being said, we are not yet through questioning. There are probably no thinking Christians who have not already asked themselves why God did not create a different world—one in which there was no evolution, no tedious development toward it, no painful advancement toward truth, but instead a creation that was already where it was meant to be, from the beginning and forever—a finished Paradise in which everything was always already present, a static world in which no guilt or failure could exist. Or we could say still more radically: why did God not just create heaven, or the world as heaven, from the beginning?

The answer can only be: in a world with no evolution, no arduous development toward God, no painful progress toward an ultimate goal, there would be no freedom. In such a world people would be mere puppets: infantile, blissful bio-machines programmed to feel happy, just as Aldous Huxley pictured them in his 1932 novel *Brave New World*.

There are some who would like to make compromises here. They say: "Certainly, God would not have needed to place us in heaven directly, but God could have created a world in which things are better ordered, in which the wielders of force are punished immediately or very soon, in which the good are rewarded and evil is visibly and obviously judged. It would be a world in which there are no dark mysteries but only clarity, transparency, and justice. There could still be freedom in such a world: the freedom to choose the good. Thus people would immediately know what is good, be able to recognize truth without obstacles and see at once how beautiful it is—and so they would also choose what is good and true. It would be a different, better world! Isn't the world that really exists a faulty design?"

No, it is not our world that is badly designed; it is this imaginary, invented world that is faulty from beginning to end! It is absurd. Should God, for example, stop violence as soon as it starts? Should the perpetrators of violence not be able to stab? Should their blades become as soft as butter when they try to use them to kill? Or should they be able to carry out the deed but then be struck by lightning so that all can see they were criminals, and as such were felled by God's punishment? It is really necessary, for once, to think through this constructed dream-world all the way to the end in order to see how unreal it is.

That world would not allow any freedom, because in *this* world freedom is always a gamble. Freedom must decide—whether to be good or not, to be genuine or not, to trust the other or not. A world with immediate sanctions would become a puppet theater, a farce, the worst kind of hokum, unworthy of God and humanity.

Freedom does not come cheaply. It is a capital that has to be earned. It can cost one's life. It is only through hard-won freedom that the human being becomes human, someone who can adore and love. Only those who are free can experience what love is.

But what about all those who have never been free? Those who, through no fault of their own, have suffered arrested development? How about those whose existence could never develop into freedom because they were severely handicapped from birth, or have had to live in inhuman conditions, or because they die as infants or when they are still embryos?

The question raised here also applies, incidentally, to the long processes that produced *Homo sapiens*. What about the billions who still lived in a state of transition—no longer entirely animal and not yet fully human? Will all those beings ultimately sink into nothingness? Into pure futility?

There is no meaningful answer to this unless we consider what we mean by "participation." It is true even for those who have become fully human that their freedom, their understanding, their dignity, even their happiness are never things that they have from or for themselves alone. One always receives these things from and with others. Eternal life, as Christians understand it, is not just an undeserved gift: beyond that it is pure participation—in the happiness, the knowledge, the freedom, the holiness of others. Ultimately it is a sharing in the life of the triune God, who is by nature community and pure participation.

This brings me to the subject of the resurrection of the dead. It was unavoidable, because for Christians there is an ultimate answer to the profound question of suffering, one that encompasses and sustains everything said to this point: the promise of resurrection. The resurrection of the dead is God's final answer to all the world's suffering.

We must not declare the path to be the goal. The goal is not yet achieved. We are still on our way to the ultimate destiny God has in mind for the world; it is called "resurrection of the dead" and, above all, of the dead who have been subjected to violence and injustice—the kind of injustice that could never be explained and never uncovered.

Still, we have to make some distinctions regarding the statement about the resurrection of the dead. Being a Christian includes an absolute confidence that the resurrection of history has already begun in the raising of Jesus: in fact, that it is already beginning now for everyone who believes in Christ. Paul and his followers, but the Gospel of John as well, put this "now already" into words when they speak of believers' daily dying and rising (Rom 6:13; 2 Cor 4:16; Col 3:1-4; John 4:24).

They speak of an experience that belongs not only to Christians but is available to everyone: those who accept their suffering, at the same time embracing it and saying a believing "yes" to it, already experience *now*, in the midst of all their pain and misery, an endless meaning that is irreducible and contains eternity.

Certainly "accepting one's suffering" must not mean only accepting *one's own*. It means, in fact, making the suffering *of others* one's own, and offering aid. That brings us back to the response to suffering in the world I have already intimated: accepting responsibility in freedom and going where our aid is needed.

In this chapter I have frequently referred to freedom. It is an essential element of human dignity. If God had created us as puppets there really would not need to be any suffering at all. Then we could live in transpersonal, infantile pleasure like what a drug trip lets us sense *in nuce*. But real happiness is something different. It always presumes freedom; it presupposes the decision of our whole existence.

Ultimately the question of how the world's suffering can coexist with God's goodness cannot be resolved by mere argument. It is a faith decision. All of us have to decide whether we prefer to believe in a perverse, unjust, senseless, and absurd world in which the suffering of the innocent, the most horrid injustice, brought upon them by human beings, goes forever unexplained—or whether we believe in a world that rests in the hands of God, the God of the Bible, who knows more than we do and has called us into freedom.

I chose the second option long ago. I refuse to regard the world and history as absurd and meaningless. I believe in the significance of creation—namely, that it will find its purpose and completion in God.

⚜

"I refuse to regard the world and history as absurd and meaningless." In that sentence I have just written I had in mind the French author and philosopher Albert Camus (1913–1960), and in no derogatory sense. I have a high regard for this existentialist because he was one of the relatively small group of agnostics who made no pretense, who looked at the world and history with astonishing sobriety, and who simply and honestly drew the consequences from the premise that we cannot count on the existence of God.

According to Albert Camus the profound suffering of the world and the misery of human life are inexplicable. Human beings are constantly seeking meaning, and yet they only find meaninglessness. In this connection Camus speaks of the "absurdity" of human existence. In his essay *The Myth of Sisyphus* he says that this absurdity, in all its merciless nakedness, can attack a person at any time, in the midst of the greyness of the everyday, on every street corner, in a tram, during a meal, in the office—posing the radical question of the "why" of everything. And this horrible senselessness of life is sealed for all time by death.

Still, Camus is not content with that analysis. He calls for opposition, rejection, fighting back, "revolt" against the absurdity of human life. However, the human "nevertheless" cannot consist in turning to some ideology, such as communism (here Camus deliberately contradicts Jean-Paul Sartre and other French existentialists). The real revolt happens in art: there the "defiant 'nevertheless'" of the human can be carried out. Art places before our eyes an image of common suffering and joy, and so it serves "revolt." It creates the world anew.

This philosophy is far from being Christianity, but in its sobriety and honesty it creates a space that makes room for further questioning. Camus was thus one of a group of thinkers that is far from small. We might call them "troubled atheists." Here I think, for example, of the French philosopher and author André Comte-Sponville (b. 1952). He was serious about the fact that even an atheist needs an ethos, one that is appropriate to herself or himself.[4] It may be derived from Christianity, from Greek philosophy, from Buddhism, and it is evident in Simone Weil.

In any case it is true that there are atheists whom every Christian can only wish to have as conversation partners. Their atheism helps such Christians to clarify their own belief and shake it free of false ballast. The encounter with an incorruptible and self-critical atheist can only enliven belief. Christian faith and a radically-questioning and concerned atheism have a great deal in common, because Jewish-Christian faith is always occupied with opposing the gods of this world and the many false images of God that constantly obscure the image of the true God. This "true enlightenment" began long ago in Israel and continues in the church. We must never forget that the early Christians were called "atheists"—that is, "godless"—by their pagan opponents for that very reason. The Russian literary scholar Mikhail Bakhtin (1895–1975), who was banished by Stalin, rightly said: "Faith borders closely on atheism; it sees and understands it. Atheism borders closely on faith and understands faith."[5]

[4] Cf. André Compte-Sponville, *Woran glaubt ein Atheist? Spiritualität ohne Gott* (Zürich: Diogenes, 2018).

[5] For a thorough discussion of Bakhtin's ideas about a "feeling for faith" and his Orthodox background see the essays in Susan M. Felch and Paul J. Contino, eds., *Bakhtin and Religion: A Feeling for Faith* (Evanston, IL: Northwestern University Press, 2001).

The true atheist understands faith because the atheist thinks and lives radically. The truly dangerous enemy of faith is therefore not atheism, but indifference, convenience, lukewarmness, apathy, arrogance—both within and outside the church.

13

Why I Believe in God

I begin this chapter—the most important one in this book—with a question we ought to reflect on very often. It is: whom can we really trust? I am not speaking of some generalized everyday trust such as we must constantly place in others because otherwise we simply could not exist.

In one way or another we are always trusting. We rely on our butcher to know that the sausage he sells us is not poisoned. We trust our dentist not to pull a healthy tooth by mistake. We expect from the driver of the BMW rushing toward us on a country road that she will not crash head-on into our car. In this sense we have to trust all day, every day.

That is not what I am getting at with the question of whom we can really trust. I am talking about that ultimate, profound trust with which I surrender my life, my whole existence, to another. I mean the trust that is full self-surrender without any reservation or condition. I mean absolute trust.

I may trust only God in that way.[1] It is only to God that I may surrender my whole life, and it is only God who may demand absolute trust from me because God is the absolute Holy One, the absolute Truth, and the absolute Good. When the Bible refers to "believing" it means this self-surrendering "trust."

[1] Cf. Romano Guardini, *Wahrheit und Ordnung 7. Das Gleichnis vom Säemann (Universitätspredigten)* (Würzburg: Fränksche Gesellschaftsdruckerei, 1956), 159–80, at 163–65.

Still, when I say that only God is the absolutely Holy One, the absolute Truth, the One who is absolutely beneficent, and God is the only one in whom I can trust without condition, I am at the same time saying that God has a face. God is personal. If I believe in God, then I believe not in a thing, certainly not in doctrines, not even in "Absolute Being" or the "First Cause." Rather, I believe in a person. It is only to a person that I can completely surrender myself, and I can only do that toward a person who looks at me, speaks to me, wants me, loves me. (Caution: I have already said in Chapter 7 that we may not understand the idea of divine persons as identical with our usual concept of persons.)

The Old Testament itself says that God is person. Of course, it does not use the word "person." *As a term*, that word only entered theological usage at a later time. But what "person" means appears a thousandfold in the Old Testament, especially in the Psalms. God looks at people. God speaks. God acts. God gives. God turns away. God is angry. God forgets that anger. God forgives. God consoles. God wipes the tears from human eyes. All these anthropomorphisms that speak as if God were a human being are ultimately meant to say that God has a face, is a person.

Still, now comes the "but." God is person, indeed. But I want to be able to see, hear, feel a person. I want to encounter the person—and that I cannot do. "No one has seen God," says the Gospel of John (John 1:18). "God dwells in unapproachable light," says 1 Timothy (1 Tim 6:16), and it adds that this is the one "whom no one has ever seen or can see."

It is only when we take seriously this ultimate hiddenness of God that we get a sense of the outrageousness of the Christian confession that God became a human being, that God's *logos* became flesh in Jesus (John 1:14), and that when we see Jesus we likewise see the Father (John 14:9). In the face of Jesus we see the face of God, and the absolute and unconditional trust of which I have spoken, that we can offer only to God, can be directed to Jesus. We may give everything over to him: our whole existence.

That God has a face, that *in Jesus* that face of the hidden God looks at us, and that in Jesus we may place our absolute trust in God—this is one of the loveliest mysteries of Christianity. Why is this mystery so profound, so moving, so incomparable? Why does it surpass everything that the world's many religions possess?

It is because in the mystery of the incarnation God remains the Hidden One, the Ungraspable, the Immeasurable, the Untouchable, the Holy One—and because at the same time and to the same degree God is the Revealed One whose face one can see, the one who surrenders and becomes vulnerable, whose innermost heart is laid open. This divine self-surrender in Jesus defines much that makes Christian faith unique and profoundly separates it from all the world's religions. At this point I can name only the most important of these things:

For example, there is the fact that Jesus rejected every form of violence. He not only demanded that his disciples practice absolute nonviolence; he himself did not use force in any form, but always trusted in free persuasion. Jesus preferred to let himself be killed by his opponents rather than use force. That is a decisive and revealing difference from the god of Islam, the Quran, and the real practice of Muhammad. The difference must never be erased. We have to commit to it. Still better, we have to live it.[2]

The mystery of the incarnation also includes the truth that God has personally entered into history. God not only became flesh but surrendered to history. We have known since Herodotus, Thucydides, Livy, and Tacitus what "history" is. No, we already know it from the Old Testament. We know that the ahistorical nature religions, which live on the basis of constantly recurring annual cycles and the return of what is eternally the same, have not yet recognized an essential existential truth about humanity or have even erased it. As a result they cannot withstand the stare of an enlightened human being, because they do not know what history is. It is our fate. God has entered into history, radically and forever.

The mystery of the incarnation also includes the truth that God has sanctified the world. God has become flesh and has taken on everything that belongs to the world: the helpless entry of the infant into the world, struggling to breathe; its first cry; its eager

[2] That, of course, says nothing about the necessity of the state and of orderly and legitimate use of force. Without such legal force no state can exist. Certainly the Christian's duty is different from that of the state. See, at length, Gerhard Lohfink, *Wem gilt die Bergpredigt? Beiträge zu einer christlichen Ethik* (Freiburg: Herder, 1988).

and yet tedious learning; the sicknesses, the enmities, and in the end, death. God not only became human but became a Jew, and in that Jewishness God became world. Thus is the world made holy, and thus every religion that preaches "flight from the world" and "otherworldliness" or that regards every desire as negative has become an outlier (I am thinking, of course, of Buddhism). We may desire. We may desire everything good and true and beautiful, as long as it happens within the order of creation. We may love passionately. We may rejoice in creation and taste of it.

Finally, the mystery of the incarnation includes the truth that God has endowed the world with an unconquerable hope: for if God not only created the world but has *become* world, then this world must have a goal—an all-surpassing future that absorbs even suffering and misery into the divine glory. It is a vision that pushes aside all views of the world that despair at the suffering in the world and then wrest a heroic "nevertheless" from their despair.

My readers will long since have noticed that my reflections in this chapter on the incarnation of God are at the same time a quarrel with the gigantic world of the religions and world philosophies. Of course it is all rather broad-brush. It could not be otherwise in a limited space. But behind it is a constant dialogue between me and the dissonant voices in our society, and an uninterrupted dispute with the world religions. The *Integrierte Gemeinde,* for as long as I have known it, has contended with both. Our views of society and of the religions have held us in suspense—not as aloof observers but as those who are forced to deal with the questions that constantly drive our society to and fro. That contention has not damaged my faith: on the contrary. I hope it has become more realistic and profound than it was in its early years.

With that I am approaching the conclusion of this chapter. The phrase "why I believe in God" is basically unsatisfactory and one-sided. The book's title really should be: "*Why I believe in the God I recognize in Jesus Christ*." And even that would not be enough. I can really only know Jesus *in the Holy Spirit he has given us,* so as not to leave us alone—and indeed *in that Holy Spirit that gives life to the church and moves it forward*. The Apostles' Creed summarizes all that in its three articles, and it all really belongs in the book's title. But giving a book its title is difficult—often the most difficult thing about it.

Still, the true, inexpressible title is at least named here, and I can finally come to my book's most important statement: *Why Do I Believe In God?*

I believe in God because God has come to meet me in Jesus Christ, and meets me again and again. God meets me in Sacred Scripture, that indescribable book in which no one ever comes to the end. But God also encounters me in the many sisters and brothers who entrust themselves to the church, *even though* there is so much sin in it. At least it *confesses* its guilt, every Sunday and in every Mass. Besides that, it contains countless saints, who are the church's true miracle. Those who despise the church are only fixated on its guilt and its mistakes. They look away; they do not recognize all the goodness and beauty that live in it.

I cannot turn away. I look at the many, many people who have met me in the church and who continue to meet me again and again, helping me and bringing me joy. But above all I look at Jesus. To him I hold fast. In him I will die.

14

Does That Say It All?

Why do I believe in God? Have I really said everything I have to say? Probably there are many other things, besides what I have expressed here, that make me believe in the church and its message about Jesus Christ, gladly and with all my heart.

Is it, perhaps, the fascination of a Gregorian chorale, with its plaintiveness and its hope?

Is it the beauty of the ancient images of Mary in which solidity of form and medieval faith find a unity that can never be reproduced?

Is it Jesus' parables and the incomparable impact of his Sermon on the Mount?

Or is it the way the Psalms bring me joy, day after day, and give me answers to the questions I ask God?

Is it because the sacrament of penance exists: the final judgment brought into the present, a downpayment on redemption?

Is it because Christian faith contains and saturates *everything*: life and death, nature and history, guilt and redemption—star and flower, spirit and garment, love, suffering, and time and eternity?[1]

Or is it simply the splendor of reality?

From time to time I open an old prayer book. It has always been precious to me because my mother used it nearly every day. Once

[1] Drawing on Clemens Brentano's poem, "Was reif in diesen Zeilen steht."

I found, as I paged through it, that on the last page, in her clear and beautiful script, she had written: "We have nothing that we have not received. All is grace."[2]

[2] Cf. 1 Cor 4:7. My mother probably recalled "all is grace" directly or indirectly from George Bernanos's novel, *Diary of a Country Priest*, where these are the last words of the young *Curé*.

Afterword

Gerhard Lohfink dedicated his last book to his teacher, Rudolf Schnackenburg. I am now writing the Afterword to the American edition of that book as Gerhard Lohfink's student, at the request of the translator, herself a student of the same teacher. As Gerhard Lohfink entered into his professorship in Tübingen in the winter semester of 1973/74, I began my own studies in theology in that same university. In Chapter 10 of this book the author describes the circumstances of his first lecture on "Text, Canon, and Hermeneutics." I still remember it clearly, because it was also the first lecture I attended on the subject of the New Testament. He presented what was needed, all of it in his usual level and composed way. There was no trace of the agitation brought upon him by the sudden summons to a welcome from the president of the university, in whose outer office he hastily sketched out the last part of his lecture. I only learned of it from this book.

Gerhard Lohfink was never fazed, even under the utmost pressure. His book *Wie hat Jesus Gemeinde gewollt* (published in English as *Jesus and Community*), the first that made him truly prominent, was based on long, thorough groundwork, but the final manuscript was produced under the pressure of a deadline. It went this way: the Master wrote the text overnight, in his clear, clean hand. In the morning the efficient secretary typed it, and in the afternoon the Assistant and student helpers corrected it. The Master took the correction process very seriously. When the proofs arrived he, as usual, summoned a book dealer he especially valued because of her special charism of finding typos. I still remember very clearly the day when the first package of freshly printed copies was delivered to the office. The assistant and student helpers happened to be in a conference with the professor. He took a copy of the book out of the box and opened it somewhere in the middle; his first glance found a typo. When I advised him to include the incident in this book, he refused: "That is not important enough!" Such reasoning was characteristic of him: he was always about what was important, and for that very reason he was always diligent about accuracy, precision, and correctness.

The Assistant always had to keep a written record of oral exams. That could produce a variety of surprises, but here again the Master always remained calm, even when a student interpreting 1 Corinthians 15:5 confused Cephas and Caiaphas and could not say exactly who either of them was. It was Gerhard Lohfink's custom to begin every exam with a brief text the student was supposed to have prepared, in Greek. It was drawn from a short list that had been given to the student. One day the examinee was asked to deal with the prescript of the letter to Titus. He explained that he had not prepared that text, and asked if he might use another. After a moment's reflection the professor answered that he wanted to stay with the text he had proposed: the student should translate it and then say something about it on the basis of his general knowledge. I held my breath. But the student showed that he really knew an astonishing amount. Afterward there was discussion of a number of other topics, and in the end the student received an A (a "1" in the German system). I asked Gerhard, after the exam, why he had not just changed the topic. He answered: "I was aware that he knows a lot, and I wanted to give him an A. If I had left the first question unanswered, that would not have been possible."

In his last book Gerhard also mentions the contributions of many students, women and men, who wrote their senior theses or master's essays for him. "Obviously I assigned them topics that were of burning interest to me," he writes. But he could make generous exceptions. I wanted to develop philological themes, both in my master's essay and my dissertation. That led the theology faculty to criticize my dissertation as not being in any way theological. Still, in the end it was accepted. When it came to the subject of my *Habilitation*, my *Doktorvater* was clear: now I had to develop a genuinely theological theme. We went for a walk, and on the way he suggested three possible topics. I spontaneously chose "Jesus' preaching on judgment." It was a subject that had not enjoyed much interest; then as now it was a thoroughly unpopular but undoubtedly important theme. After about two years of work I arrived at a point where I saw no way forward. It was unclear to me how I could make the transition from early Jewish ideas of judgment to Jesus' preaching. I wrote Gerhard in despair, saying I would have to give up. The following day he came to our house and showed me how I could proceed, drawing in simple graphics on paper the eschatological models of Early Judaism I had developed. He liked to use such graphics in his lectures, especially because he was good at drawing. That overcame my mental block. I am grateful to him for the graphics, which appeared in the published book; it was translated by Linda Maloney and published in America as *Jesus and Judgment* (Fortress, 1990), with the graphics included.

Gerhard Lohfink's lectures usually took place in the largest auditorium of the "Kupferbau." They were attended not only by Roman Catholic theology students but also by Protestants. The reason was not only that he was noted for his personal integrity and devotion to truth—the same was true of the exegetes then teaching in the Protestant faculty (Otto Betz, Hartmut Gese, Martin Hengel, Otfried Hofius, Peter Stuhlmacher). It was, above all, because his lectures were so easy to follow. The topics were well prepared, with appropriate examples; the thought was orderly, and everything was structured in a relatable way. He even used to dictate "key sentences" or phrases, always short and clear, for students to memorize—an old-fashioned way of teaching. So also in exams: you knew what to expect. But order was not only characteristic of his thinking; it was part of his being. When he came to the office in the morning he inevitably arranged all the pens and pencils on his desk horizontally and vertically. He was indeed, as Germans say, "in Ordnung."

The Master used to gather students who were writing theses or dissertations for him in his "Oberseminar" (Graduate Seminar); there we took turns reporting on our research. In the summer semester the seminar met for a short hike in the woods, usually leading to a small shelter where we grilled sausages. Once we went punting on the River Neckar, which flows through Tübingen.

In the winter semester the Assistant invited everyone to his home during the Christmas season.

In the hectic time when the dogmatics professor Hans Küng had his *missio canonica* withdrawn and therefore had to leave the Catholic faculty, it happened that Gerhard Lohfink, having been "Dekan" (similar to "Dean") the previous year, was "Prodekan" ("vice dean") of the faculty. When he had reached that point in the chapter about Tübingen in this, his last book, he asked me in one of our long telephone conversations whether and how he should treat that affair in his book. I suggested that he could write a few sentences about it in his usual diplomatic language, correcting certain misunderstandings. As the reader has seen, he omitted the matter entirely. Miserable quarrels that seldom proceed without unjust accusations from both sides were simply not his thing.

Gerhard Lohfink ultimately left the faculty and the university of his own accord. His statement in this book that he "left university service" in the year 1986 might be misunderstood. It means that he resigned his professorship in that year so that the opening could be published. But he retained the position until his successor arrived, and continued to teach for two more semesters. The book explains his reasons for taking this unusual step. The memorable farewell lecture whose beginning is quoted in this book, with the great reception that followed it, took place on July 6, 1987. It was a horribly hot day. None of the guests at the reception wanted to drink wine; they opted for cold water and juice!

Gerhard's students and assistants from his Tübingen years also gave him a little farewell party at which we presented him with a privately-produced volume of personal essays as a "little thank-you gift." I want to quote part of the Foreword: "We have certainly learned much from you about scholarship and research, as well as the judiciousness, accuracy, and meticulousness they demand. But we have learned far more from you about the attitude and goals with which we should 'search the scriptures' (cf. John 5:39). We admire and treasure your honesty and modesty, your seriousness and sense of consequence: all of them are consequential for discipleship."

Anyone who simply glances at the list of Gerhard Lohfink's publications will quickly notice the quality and scope of the "judiciousness" with which he conducted his exegesis of the New Testament. He not only included consideration of the Old Testament—for which he could draw on his brother's expertise—but also philosophical and theological contexts and questions belonging to natural science. Drawing on this broad intellectual horizon, he could approach exegetical questions much more appropriately and accurately than is usually the case with purely historical-critical exegesis. On that basis he was able to write the impressive chapter in this book that he calls "Defending God." The chapter that follows it, "Why I Believe in God," he himself calls "the most important in this book." It is a confession of the Incarnation and of Jesus.

He died as he had lived. On Maundy Thursday 2024 he engaged in the final discussion of this book with the academic editor at Herder, Dr. Bruno Steimer. On Good Friday a Mass was celebrated at his bedside and, at his request, the whole Passion account was read. On Holy Saturday he received the anointing of the sick. He died on Easter Tuesday. His burial service at the Waldfriedhof in Munich, designed and conducted by his friends from the *Integrierte Gemeinde*, was one of the loveliest I have attended. *Requiescat in pace!*

Marius Reiser

Acknowledgments

Memory is a funny thing. When you start to look back at your life you are amazed at what arises out of the bottomless well of the past. Still, some figures surface that you cannot really trust, and memories of words you are not sure about. Is memory playing games with us? So we ask for help. We ask other people; we implore them to remember with us.

For this assistance in remembering I want to give most sincere thanks here—first to my brother Norbert, who reviewed the whole manuscript; then to Gerd Block, who also read the whole thing closely; also to my fellow student at the Heinrich-von-Gagern Gymnasium, Barbara Scardigli; then to my former student Hans Josef Miller (he it was who so sharply dismissed the occupiers from the lecture hall); and obviously my then-assistant in Tübingen, Marius Reiser, who remembered during our many, many telephone calls things that had completely escaped me.

I also thank Johannes Hamel, to whose sharp eyes I entrusted some central texts of the manuscript, and Hans Hubert Klein, who gave me crucial assistance with the list of my publications that follows, and finally my dear housemates Carmelita and Gerd Block, with whom I sit at table day after day.

But there were also many others with whom, in these last months, I have spoken about things from years past: above all Achim Buckenmaier, who helped in our community in Tanzania for such a long time, and whose advice about church dogmatics I value to the highest degree.

As always, my thanks go to Dr. Bruno Steimer from the theology section of Herder. We have been in constant contact and he has advised and supported me in a way I will never forget. Those thanks are due also to the whole of the Herder publishing house for many kinds of help—and especially to Francesca Bressan in the Foreign Rights department, who sees to the translation and publication of my books throughout the world.

As regards my computer problems: why do the programmers make their systems ever more complicated and incomprehensible? For this book, as for others, Raphael Jaklitsch repeatedly delivered me from my dilemmas, with full knowledge and a sure hand. Hans Pachner, too, faithfully brought me books from the Bavarian State Library. He, together with Gerd Block and Raphael Jaklitsch, have been my indispensable emergency corps.*

The joy and affection with which I write these acknowledgments are, of course, due to my readers. I feel connected with all of you. God bless you, wherever you are!

Gerhard Lohfink †
(1934–2024)

*Gerhard Lohfink customarily also thanked, in U.S. editions, Liturgical Press and its directors, Peter Dwyer and Therese Ratliff, and editorial director Hans Christoffersen. He would have done so also for this, his twelfth book with Liturgical Press, had he lived. Shortly before his death he wrote to the Rev. Dr. Linda Maloney: "I could never have found a translator with such extraordinary qualifications in theology and biblical studies. Therefore again and emphatically: many, many, many thanks." It should be said that she has those qualifications only because she was Gerhard Lohfink's doctoral student.

Books by Gerhard Lohfink

Books translated into English, by date:

The Gospels: God's Word in Human Words. Chicago: Franciscan Herald Press, 1972. [Partial translation.]
Original: *Die Bibel: Gotteswort in Menschenwort*. Stuttgart: Katholisches Bibelwerk, 1967.

The Conversion of St. Paul: Narrative and History in Acts. Translated and edited by Bruce J. Malina. Herald Scriptural Library. Chicago: Franciscan Herald Press, 1976.
Original: *Paulus vor Damaskus. Arbeitsweisen der neueren Bibelwissenschaft dargestellt an den Texten Apg 9,1-19; 22:3-21; 26:9-18*. SBS 4. Stuttgart: Katholisches Bibelwerk, 1965.

Death Is Not the Final Word. Translated by Robert J. Cunningham. Chicago: Franciscan Herald Press, 1977.
Original: *Der Tod ist nicht das letzte Wort. Meditationen*. Freiburg: Herder, 1976.

The Bible: Now I Get It! A Form-Criticism Handbook. Translated by Daniel Coogan. Illustrated by Bill Woodman. New York: Doubleday, 1979.
Original: *Jetzt verstehe ich die Bibel. Ein Sachbuch zur Formkritik*. Stuttgart: Katholisches Bibelwerk, 1973.

The Last Day of Jesus: An Enriching Portrayal of the Passion. Translated by Salvator Attanasio. Notre Dame, IN: Ave Maria Press, 1984.
Original: *Der letzte Tag Jesu. Die Ereignisse der Passion*. Freiburg: Herder, 1981. Repr. as *Der letzte Tag Jesu. Was bei der Passion wirklich geschah*. Stuttgart: Katholisches Bibelwerk, 2005.

Jesus and Community: The Social Dimension of Christian Faith. Translated by John P. Galvin. Philadelphia: Fortress Press; New York: Paulist Press, 1984.
Original: *Wie hat Jesus Gemeinde gewollt? Zur gesellschaftlichen Dimension des christlichen Glaubens*. Freiburg: Herder, 1982. New, revised and

expanded ed., *Wie hat Jesus Gemeinde gewollt? Kirche im Kontrast*. Stuttgart: Katholisches Bibelwerk, 2015.

The Work of God Goes On. Translated by Linda M. Maloney. Philadelphia: Fortress Press, 1987.

Original: *Gottes Taten gehen weiter. Geschichtstheologie als Grundvollzug neutestamentlicher Gemeinden*. Freiburg: Herder, 1985.

Does God Need the Church? Toward a Theology of the People of God. Translated by Linda M. Maloney. Collegeville, MN: Liturgical Press, 1999.

Original: *Braucht Gott die Kirche? Zur Theologie des Volkes Gottes*. Freiburg: Herder; Hagen: Verlag Urfeld, 1998.

Jesus of Nazareth: What He Wanted, Who He Was. Translated by Linda M. Maloney. Collegeville, MN: Liturgical Press, 2012.

Original: *Jesus von Nazaret: Was er wollte, wer er war*. Freiburg: Herder, 2011.

No Irrelevant Jesus: On Jesus and the Church Today. Translated by Linda M. Maloney. Collegeville, MN: Liturgical Press, 2014.

Original: *Gegen die verharmlosung Jesu. Reden über Jesus und die Kirche*. Freiburg: Herder, 2013; special ed. 2022.

The Our Father: A New Reading. Translated by Linda M. Maloney. Collegeville, MN: Liturgical Press, 2018.

Original: *Das Vaterunser – neu ausgelegt*. Urfelder Reihe 7. Bad Tölz: Verlag Urfeld, 2007. New ed. Stuttgart: Katholisches Bibelwerk 2012.

Is This All There Is? On Resurrection and Eternal Life. Translated by Linda M. Maloney. Collegeville, MN: Liturgical Press, 2018.

Original: *Am Ende das Nichts? Über Auferstehung und ewiges Leben*. Freiburg: Herder, 2017; special ed. 2024.

The Forty Parables of Jesus. Translated by Linda M. Maloney. Collegeville, MN: Liturgical Press, 2021.

Original: *Die vierzig Gleichnisse Jesu*. Freiburg: Herder, 2020.

Prayer Takes Us Home: The Theology and Practice of Christian Prayer. Translated by Linda M. Maloney. Collegeville, MN: Liturgical Press, 2022.

Original: *Beten schenkt Heimat. Theologie und Praxis des christlichen Gebets*. Freiburg: Herder, 2010.

Between Heaven and Earth: New Explorations of Great Biblical Texts. Translated by Linda M. Maloney. Collegeville, MN: Liturgical Press, 2022.

Original: *Ausgespannt zwischen Himmel und Erde. Große Bibeltexte neu erkundet*. Freiburg: Herder, 2021.

The Christian Faith Explained in Fifty Letters. Translated by Christopher Groß. New York and Mahwah, NJ: Paulist Press, 2022.
Original: *Der christliche Glaube erklärt in 50 Briefen*. Freiburg: Herder, 2018.

The Most Important Words of Jesus. Translated by Linda M. Maloney. Collegeville, MN: Liturgical Press, 2023.
Original: *Die wichtigsten Worte Jesu*. Freiburg: Herder, 2022.

All My Springs Are in You: More Explorations of Great Biblical Texts. Translated by Linda M. Maloney. Collegeville, MN: Liturgical Press, 2024.
Original: *All meine Quellen entspringen in dir. Große Bibeltexte neu erkundet*. Freiburg: Herder, 2023.

Other books, not in English:

Die Himmelfahrt Jesu. Untersuchungen zu den Himmelfahrts- und Erhöhungstexten bei Lukas. SANT 26. Munich: Kösel, 1971.

Die Himmelfahrt Jesu — Erfindung oder Erfahrung? Kleine Reihe zur Bibel 1. Stuttgart: Katholisches Bibelwerk, 1972; 3rd ed. 1986.

Gott ohne Masken. Predigten und Ansprachen. Würzburg: Echter, 1972.

Die Sammlung Israels. Eine Untersuchung zur lukanischen Ekklesiologie. SANT 39. Munich: Kösel, 1975.

Naherwartung – Auferstehung – Unsterblichkeit. With Gisbert Greshake. QD 71. Freiburg: Herder, 1975; 3rd expanded ed., 1978; 5th expanded ed., 1986.

Der Tod ist nicht das letzte Wort. Meditationen. Freiburg: Herder, 1976. Published under the same title by Verlag der action 365 (Frankfurt), 2009.

Glaube braucht Erfahrung. Würzburg: Echter, 1977.

Bittgebet — Testfall des Glaubens. Ed. with Gisbert Greshake. Includes contributions by Gisbert Greshake, Anselm Hertz, Gerhard Lohfink, Thomas Pröpper, and Hans Schaller. Mainz: Grünewald, 1978.

Tiefenpsychologie und keine Exegese. Eine Auseinandersetzung mit Eugen Drewermann. With Rudolf Pesch. SBS 129. Stuttgart: Katholisches Bibelwerk, 1987.

Studien zum Neuen Testament. SBAB NT 5. Stuttgart: Katholisches Bibelwerk, 1989.

Gottes Volksbegehren. Biblische Herausforderungen. Munich: Neue Stadt, 1998.

Die Feier des Sonntags. Auslegungen der Schrifttexte. Lesejahr A. Ed. Gerhard Lohfink, Rudolf Pesch, and Ludwig Weimer. Bad Tölz: Verlag Urfeld, 2001.

Die Feier des Sonntags. Auslegungen der Schrifttexte. Lesejahr B. Ed. Gerhard Lohfink, Rudolf Pesch, and Ludwig Weimer. Bad Tölz: Verlag Urfeld, 2002.

Die Feier des Sonntags. Auslegungen der Schrifttexte. Lesejahr C. Ed. Gerhard Lohfink, Rudolf Pesch, and Ludwig Weimer. Bad Tölz: Verlag Urfeld, 2003.

Auf der Erde, wo sonst? Ein theologisches Tagebuch. Bad Tölz: Verlag Urfeld, 2003. Updated edition with new subtitle, ***Unangepasstes über Gott und die Welt.*** Stuttgart: Katholisches Bibelwerk, 2015.

Bibel Ja – Kirche Nein? Kriterien richtiger Bibelauslegung. Urfelder Texte 1. Bad Tölz: Verlag Urfeld, 2004.

Am ersten Tag der Woche. Auslegungen der Schrifttexte. Lesejahr B. Edited with Bernhard Koch and Ludwig Weimer. Stuttgart: Katholisches Bibelwerk; Bad Tölz: Verlag Urfeld, 2006.

Maria – nicht ohne Israel. Eine neue Sicht der Lehre von der Unbefleckten Empfängnis. With Ludwig Weimer. Freiburg: Herder, 2008; new ed., 2012; 3rd ed., 2017.

Welche Argumente hat der neue Atheismus? Eine kritische Auseinandersetzung. Urfelder Reihe 8. Bad Tölz: Verlag Urfeld, 2008. New, revised ed.: ***Der neue Atheismus. Eine kritische Auseinandersetzung.*** Stuttgart: Katholisches Bibelwerk, 2013.

Heute – wann sonst? Unangepasstes über Gott und die Welt. Stuttgart: Katholisches Bibelwerk, 2014.

Das Geheimnis des Galiläers. Ein Nachtgespräch über Jesus von Nazaret. Freiburg: Herder, 2019.

Scripture Index*

* Does not include passages referred to in the footnotes.